BACK TO BASICS

A Study of the Second Lebanon War and Operation CAST LEAD

Lieutenant Colonel Scott C. Farquhar
General Editor

Combat Studies Institute Press
US Army Combined Arms Center (CAC)
Fort Leavenworth, Kansas

Library of Congress Cataloging-in-Publication Data

Back to basics : a study of the second Lebanon War and Operation CAST LEAD / Scott C. Farquhar, general editor.

p. cm.

ISBN 978-0-9823283-3-0

1. Israel--Military policy. 2. Gaza War, 2008-2009. 3. Lebanon War, 2006--Influence. 4. Israel. Tseva haganah le-Yisra'el--Drill and tactics. 5. Harakat al-Muqawamah al-Islamiyah. 6. Hizballah (Lebanon) I. Farquhar, Scott C. II. Title.

DS119.767.B33 2009

956.9405'4--dc22

2009015841

First printing, May 2009

Foreword

The Israeli incursions into Lebanon in mid-2006 and into Gaza in late 2008/early 2009 are important studies in contrasts. During the first, often termed "the Second Lebanon War," Hezbollah fought Israeli Defense Forces (IDF) seeking hostage rescue and retribution to a bloody standstill. During the second, Hamas enjoyed far less success against the same forces avowedly in pursuit of only self-defense.

These and other differences notwithstanding, the two conflicts are both similar and linked in several important respects. Each witnessed protagonists that were anxious—even desperate—to win prestige and demonstrate the capacity to safeguard survival. Each also confronted a conventional armed force with antagonists, Hezbollah and Hamas, which are possible prototypes for the non-state adversaries the US could face in the future. Moreover, each conflict witnessed the successful prosecution of information operations in ways that highlighted the importance of the "new media" in contemporary war. At the same time, the conflicts were linked intellectually, to the extent that the IDF studied lessons learned from the first, especially in the realm of information operations, to condition planning and application for the second.

The current work metaphorically extends IDF lessons learned to distill insights from the two conflicts for the education of US Army leaders. Produced in a short period of time, this anthology represents the collaborative effort of several organizations, including CAC's Center for Army Lessons Learned, the Combat Studies Institute, the US Army's Information Operations Proponent, the Command and General Staff College, and TRADOC's Intelligence Support Activity. Relying on a mixture of primary and secondary materials from a variety of sources and agencies, the authors have combined multiple perspectives under the roof of a single unclassified study. Like the classics, it reaffirms the importance of basics and constant introspection as important prerequisites for military success.

William B. Caldwell, IV
Lieutenant General, US Army
Commanding

Contents

Introduction

Recently the *Economist* magazine referred to the Arab-Israeli conflicts as "The Hundred Years' War" in its coverage of the Israeli Defense Forces' assault on Hamas in the Gaza Strip during Operation CAST LEAD. Comparing this seemingly intractable ethno-sectarian conflict to Europe's fratricidal wars is taking the long view and is apt to explain it to interested readers. This study does not try to encapsulate the origins nor predict the future of this long and on-going conflict; instead it examines the combat actions in two of the most recent operations in Lebanon and the Gaza Strip. The common denominator in these fights is the Israeli Defense Forces (IDF). Consequently the writing team focused on the impact that transformation had on this military organization before and after the Second Lebanon War of 2006 and in preparation for Operation CAST LEAD in the winter of 2008-09. The methodology and composition of the IDF's enemies, Hezbollah and Hamas, are studied as well.

The adaptations that the IDF made in anticipation of future conflict after the period following the withdrawal from southern Lebanon in 2000 were not made in a political or fiscal vacuum. Two earlier works by the Combat Studies Institute (CSI), *We Were Caught Unprepared: The 2006 Hezbollah-Israeli War* and *Flipside of the COIN: Israel's Lebanese Incursion Between 1982-2000*, explore some of these aspects as Israeli society attempted to reconcile a "peace dividend" from its withdrawal from the grinding and divisive occupation of southern Lebanon with the need to secure its population from the terror-bombings that accompanied the Second Intifada. The IDF also attempted to adapt new technologies and ideas into a revolutionary doctrine that would avoid the manpower-intensive, and necessarily casualty-producing, conflicts that the Jewish state abhors. The kidnapping operations by Hamas and Hezbollah ignited an Israeli retribution in the summer of 2006 before any of these adaptations were successfully promulgated, but not before its deleterious effects on the IDF had taken hold.

American professional military personnel are well-acquainted with "the arrogant show of strength" that was Task Force *Smith* in Korea in the summer of 1950 and of its fate. A similar result occurred when the vaunted IDF attacked into Lebanon in 2006 against the guerrilla army of Hezbollah: a first-world army was fought to a standstill by a tough and determined enemy despite overwhelming air power. The IDF pitted ill-trained soldiers and ill-educated officers, who attempted to carry out vague orders and unfamiliar tasks, against a small group of men with good weapons and a simple mission. This was the first open conflict in Israel's "cold war" with Iran and its proxy force of Hezbollah in what became known as the Second Lebanon War.

1

In the first chapter, a narrative of the two operations from the Israeli point of view explains the combat actions and the important reforms made by the IDF between them. CSI historian Matt Matthews used interviews of IDF personnel to gain an insight into his synthesis of professional analysis and military and commercial journalism. This chapter is one of the first and most comprehensive open-source explorations of the battles in Lebanon and Gaza, as well as the low-level struggle within the IDF over its doctrine between the conflicts.

The period that followed the Second Lebanon War war was as acrimonious and recriminatory to the IDF and Israel as was Vietnam to the US Army and American society; truncated in both scale and scope as Israel is a small country without comforting oceans or benign neighbors on its flanks. Matthews captures the series of clear-eyed panels that set to work in the IDF to study the Second Lebanon War while a similar commission did the same for the political apparatus. In a very short amount of time, the IDF took the panels' recommendations and placed them into effect while the political reforms remained unproven until the late winter of 2008. The ability of Hezbollah to transmit its lessons learned against the IDF to Hamas proved to be unsuccessful.

The IDF Operation CAST LEAD against Hamas in 2008-09 was a small-scale affair in comparison to the multi-division attack into Lebanon in 2006. The former operation, however, restored confidence in both the government and armed forces in the eyes of the Israeli populace. The reforms of the year and a half between conflicts paid great dividends to Israeli soldiers and aircrews. It also demonstrated Israeli resolve, created a schism in the Muslim Middle East and is only one of a series of escalations in what is becoming a very dangerous conflict in the region.

Ms. Penny Mellies' chapter is an in-depth view of Israel's enemies in Lebanon and Gaza using the US Army's doctrinal methodology to evaluate an environment. Ms. Mellies' analysis will be valuable to the interested reader who wants to understand the nature of Hezbollah and Hamas. It also serves as an example of using the doctrinal tenets to describe an operational environment. This provides instructors or students a step-by-step "how-to" use of doctrine through a useful historical analysis that is part of CSI's charter.

In addition to Mr. Matthews's historical narrative of the IDF in Lebanon and Gaza, LTC Abe Marrero examines the role and importance of doctrine to tactical leaders and formations. The dangers of unclear or incomplete doctrinal thinking and practices were clearly felt in the former conflict and the IDF's remedy in 2007 gives this work its title of "back to basics." LTC Marrero also examines how the return and adherence to sound doctrinal principles was put into effect by the IDF in Operation CAST LEAD. He also examines some of the tactical and technical innovations used by the Israeli ground and air forces in this brief fight.

LTC Michael Snyder examines the controversial and much-discussed phenomena of "information operations" in the last chapter of this study. He provides a thorough discussion of the information background and the competing narratives used by and against Israel. This chapter explains these narratives relative effectiveness on their intended (and unintended) audiences. Like Ms. Mellies, LTC Snyder is able to place doctrine into a historical context and incorporate several actual events into clear and understandable vignettes for the general or military reader. He also explains the little-known reforms that Israel made to its government to enact public diplomacy and how these were enacted in Operation CAST LEAD.

The Combat Studies Institute was able to quickly produce a collaborative comparative analysis of these conflicts, their belligerents, and lessons applicable to the US Army. This special study, *Back to Basics*, is the latest of CSI's publications on the ongoing conflicts that occur in our world and is presented as the work of the Combined Arms Center's varied expertise to its audience in the Training and Doctrine Command and the US Army.

Scott C. Farquhar
Lieutenant Colonel, US Army
General Editor

Chapter 1

Hard Lessons Learned

A Comparison of the 2006 Hezbollah-Israeli War and Operation CAST LEAD: A Historical Overview

by
Matt M. Matthews
Combat Studies Institute

Within hours of the first Israeli air strikes against Hamas on 27 December 2008, military leaders, analysts, pundits and the media began to speculate about the ability of the Israeli Defense Force (IDF) to conduct a successful campaign in Gaza. A mere two days into the operation, as the Israeli Air Force (IAF) continued to pummel terrorist targets in Gaza, some within the Israeli media were already suggesting that "the army had no appetite for a ground war."[1] This apprehension and speculation at the onset of Israeli operations against Hamas was undeniably a direct result of the IDF's uninspiring performance during its 2006 war against Hezbollah.

As the campaign progressed however, it quickly became evident to many that these early comparisons by the media and others were incorrect. The IDF's campaign in Gaza, designated Operation CAST LEAD, would prove a far cry from the war against Hezbollah. Unlike 2006, there were no grand pronouncements of unachievable strategic goals emanating from the Israeli Prime Minister.[2] Furthermore, as the IAF demolished Hamas' leadership, training camps and weaponry in the early stages of the campaign, there were no bombastic proclamations similar to that of former Chief of the IDF General Staff, Dan Halutz, that "[w]e have won the war." It seemed as if Israeli ground forces in Gaza had undergone a major cultural change in terms of decisiveness, aggressiveness, commitment to the mission and willingness to accept casualties. In this engagement, IDF commanders led from the front, cell phones were seized from Israeli soldiers, and the media heavily restricted from access to the battlefield. In a complete reversal from 2006, the IDF reserves were promptly called to duty and arrived on the battlefield well trained and well-equipped. Quite unlike 2006, the ground campaign was judged excellent. "Up to brigade level it was a showcase, orderly, perfect execution, timely [and] disciplined, [the] reservist [are] as good as regulars," wrote one Israeli officer.[3]

The campaign against Hamas seemingly represents a dramatic turnaround by the IDF after its faltering performance against Hezbollah in southern Lebanon. How was this accomplished? Considering the major disparities in intelligence, terrain, weaponry, training and the fighting qualities of Hamas and Hezbollah, were the enhancements made by the IDF really all that significant? This chapter will provide a concise history of the 2006 Hezbollah-Israeli war, (for which I have borrowed heavily from my *Long War Series Occasional Paper 26—We Were Caught Unprepared: The 2006 Hezbollah-Israeli War*), examine the problems faced by the IDF during the conflict and its resulting overhaul in the intervening two years between the war with Hezbollah and examine the campaign against Hamas. This chapter will also address the events surrounding the IDF's recent incursion into Gaza and evaluate the differences between the two campaigns.

The 2006 Hezbollah-Israeli War

When Hezbollah fighters ambushed and killed three Israeli reserve soldiers and kidnapped two others on 12 July 2006, near Zarit, Israel, the incident sparked a 33-day war that would expose major problems within the IDF. The ensuing conflict would also mark Hezbollah as a bold, astute and resourceful adversary. By the summer of 2006, Hezbollah had assembled a well-trained, well-armed, highly motivated, and highly evolved war-fighting machine on Israel's northern border. Hezbollah had managed to drive the Israelis out of southern Lebanon in 2000, in a masterful 18-year campaign that proved an embarrassing defeat for the IDF, its first. During the ensuing years, Hezbollah set about transforming itself from a purely guerrilla army into what its Secretary-General, Hasan Nasrallah, called a "new model" army. "It was not a regular army but was not a guerrilla in the traditional sense either. It was something in between," Nasrallah stated.[4]

It would appear that a major portion of Hezbollah's operational design was based on the presumption that Israel no longer had a tolerance for war and its inevitable butcher's bill. In fact, Hezbollah Secretary-General Hasan Nasrallah stated in his victory speech on 26 May 2000, in the newly liberated town of Bint Jbeil, that "Israeli society is as weak as a spider web." Nasrallah was convinced that "the Israeli Achilles heel" was, "Israeli society itself."

The Hezbollah Secretary-General was certain "that Israeli society is a brittle post-military society that cannot endure wars anymore and that under pressure it can succumb to Arab aggression." Building on this premise, Hezbollah was convinced that in any future war Israel would rely heavily on air and artillery precision weapons, and limit its use of ground forces. These operational hypotheses were based on Hezbollah's experiences in its first long war with Israel. It was confident that Israel would have no stomach for casualties in any future conflict, and would conduct the majority of its operations using standoff-based firepower. Available historic evidence appears to indicate this rationale was crucial as Hezbollah began its operational and tactical planning.[5]

It was imperative that Hezbollah's combat operations penetrate well inside Israel's border and not yield to the IDF's massive precision firepower. To accomplish this task, Hezbollah formed several rocket artillery units between 2000 and 2006. South of the Litani River, Hezbollah organized the Nasser unit which would control a vast arsenal of 122-mm Katyusha rockets that would be used to strike within Israel. To undermine any attempt by Israel to decimate Hezbollah's firepower with retaliatory (or pre-emptive) air strikes, the Nasser unit's missile launchers were emplaced inside the hilltop villages and towns and the surrounding orchards and fields of southern Lebanon.[6]

Hezbollah established a simple yet effective system for firing the Katyusha rockets in the face of Israeli firepower. Once lookouts declared the area free of Israeli aircraft or UAVs, a small group moved to the launch site, set up the launcher, and quickly departed. A second group would then transport the rocket to the launch location and promptly disperse. A third small squad would then arrive at the launch position and prepare the rocket for firing, often using remotely controlled or timer-based mechanisms. The entire process was to take less than 28 seconds with many of the rocket squads riding mountain bicycles to and from their positions. The vast majority of the rocket systems were cached in underground shelters and bunkers built to withstand precision air and artillery strikes.[7]

A second rocket artillery unit equipped with the medium-range Fajr and extended-range versions of Katyusha was placed both north and south of the Litani. Most of these larger rockets were to be fired from vehicle-mounted launchers, often a pickup truck or the ubiquitous small flatbed farm trucks of the region. Sandwiched between the Litani and Beirut, Hezbollah added two additional long-range rocket units manning the Iranian-made 610-mm Zelzal-2 and other long-range missile systems. By 2006, Iran and Syria had supplied Hezbollah with an astonishing 12,000 to 13,000 short-, medium-, and long-range ground-to-ground missiles. According to some intelligence sources, Iranian elements managed the offloading of the rockets in Lebanon and trained Hezbollah in their use.[8]

In order to protect its offensive rocket systems it was essential for Hezbollah to delay any Israeli ground attack aimed at siezing the launch sites. "Alongside these three or four rocket formations," an authority on Hezbollah stated, "was a ground array created south of the Litani based on underground tunnels and bunkers, explosives-ridden areas, and anti-tank units. This array was intended to confront ground forces to a limited extent, to stall ground incursions, and inflict as many casualties as possible, which would wear out IDF forces, slow down their progress, and allow continued rocket fire."[9] It is worth noting however, that some experts within the IDF believe Hezbollah's ground fighting force was not built separately or specifically to protect the rockets to delay an IDF ground assault, but was organic to the rocket units as part of a larger, combined arms organization.[10]

The Hezbollah fighters assigned to protect the rockets were armed and equipped with a massive array of sophisticated weaponry. Reinforced with hundreds of antitank missiles ranging from the AT-14 Kornet-E to the American made TOW, Hezbollah's veteran military personnel (many trained in Iran and Syria), were prepared to conduct elaborate antitank ambushes. Its fighters had trained extensively to integrate mortars and rockets into this lethal mix by pre-sighting suspected Israeli avenues of approach and training forward observers in proper indirect fire procedures. Mines and IEDs were expertly placed in depth throughout the southern defensive sector in order to stop Israeli mechanized forces and enable Hezbollah to mass both direct and indirect fires on their halted columns. A sturdy and technically advanced underground command and control (C^2) system was designed to help with the expedient delivery of orders to the front.[11] Evidence would also seem to suggest that Hezbollah's military commanders planned to keep firm operational control over their offensive rocket units while giving more tactical leeway to their ground troops.[12]

In the logistics arena, Hezbollah stockpiled every item it would need to prosecute the war effort south of the Litani. The supplies were secreted in well-fortified bunkers and entrenchments that were designed to withstand blistering IDF precision firepower. The defensive network built by Hezbollah and its erstwhile allies in southern Lebanon was an engineering marvel to Israeli and neutral observers.[13]

Although the Israeli intelligence community believed Hezbollah's defensive network was based on "Iranian military doctrine," another source suggests the elaborate system was based on "a defensive guerilla force organized along North Korean lines." In fact, the same source concluded that, "All the underground facilities [Hezbollah's], including arms dumps, food stocks, dispensaries for the wounded, were put in place primarily in 2003-2004 under the supervision of North Korean instructors." Evidence would furthermore suggest that the Iranian Revolutionary Guard was also heavily involved in the construction effort.[14] Intelligence sources concluded that Hezbollah was "believed to be benefiting from assistance provided by North Korean advisers, according to a July 29 report in *al-Sharq al-Awsat*. The report quotes a high-ranking Iranian Revolutionary Guards officer, who stated that North Korean advisers had assisted Hezbollah in building tunnel infrastructure, including a 25 kilometer underground tunnel."[15]

Between 2000 and 2006, Hezbollah also purportedly mastered the delicate art of counter-signals intelligence (C-SIGNET), a capability that would pay huge dividends in any future war with Israel. In the human intelligence (HUMINT) realm Hezbollah also proved highly successful. Working with Lebanese intelligence officers, Hezbollah managed to "turn" Israeli agents in southern Lebanon and dismantle a sizable Israeli spy ring. "In some small number of crucially important cases," wrote Crooke and Perry, "Hezbollah senior intelligence officials were able to 'feed back' false information on their militia's most important emplacements to Israel—with the result that Israeli target folders identified key emplacements that did not, in fact, exist."[16] It also appears likely that Hezbollah succeeded in placing its own agents in northern Israel.[17]

By the summer of 2006, Hezbollah had assembled a well-trained, well-armed, highly motivated, and highly evolved war-fighting machine on Israel's northern border. It consisted of at least an Iranian-trained, 3,000-man strong light infantry or commando brigade backed by a militia that was twice as large and overwhelmingly made up of veterans from 18-year campaign against Israel. Hezbollah had calculated accurately and had designed an organization and operational plan based on well-grounded assumptions. As reserve IAF campaign-planning officer Ron Tira pointed out, "Hezbollah designed a war in which presumably Israel could only choose which soft underbelly to expose: the one whereby it avoids a ground operation and exposes its home front vulnerability, or the one whereby it enters Lebanon and sustains the loss of soldiers in ongoing ground-based attrition with a guerilla organization. Hezbollah's brilliant trap apparently left Israel with two undesirable options."[18]

At the tactical level Hezbollah addressed the IDF's precision weapons capability by reducing its own weapons signature and target appearance time and through building hardened defensive positions. Knowing full well that the IDF desired to "generate effects" on its "systems" Hezbollah "created a network of autonomous cells with little inter-cell systemic interaction." On the strategic level Hezbollah also predicted that the IDF would attack with long-range precision weapons its strategic centers of gravity (SCOGs). To counter this, Hezbollah simply did away with them. In any future war with Israel there would be no critical strategic asset to attack.[19]

Over the course of six years, Hezbollah was able to efficiently adjust its tactics and operational design. Its planning was simple and inspired. During this time the Israelis also formulated a new doctrine. Unfortunately for Israel, this new doctrine was highly complex and would ultimately play into the hands of Hezbollah.

Within days of the kidnapping, Israeli Prime Minister Ehud Olmert declared his intent to destroy Hezbollah, rescue the kidnapped Israeli soldiers and alter the state of affairs in southern Lebanon. As Yair Evron wrote however, the goals "were entirely unrealistic and certainly unattainable through military force."[20] Ignoring what was obvious to many within the Israeli government and the IDF, Olmert turned to his Defense Minister, Amir Peretz and the Chief of the IDF General Staff, Dan Halutz, to implement a campaign plan against Hezbollah.

Unfortunately for Israel, Peretz proved inadequate for the task. A government report issued after the war stated that the Defense Minister "did not have knowledge or experience in military, political or governmental matters. He also did not have knowledge of the basic principles of using military force to achieve political goals." In the end, Olmert would be forced to rely almost entirely on Halutz, a man nearly as unprepared for a war against Hezbollah, as Peretz.[21]

Halutz faced numerous challenges as he scrambled to prepare a reasoned response to Hezbollah, two of which were of his own making. As the first IAF officer ever appointed Chief of the IDF General Staff, Halutz proved an unyielding advocate of air power and effects based operations (EBO).[22] "I maintain that we also have to part with the concept of a land battle," he proclaimed in 2001. He also maintained that "Victory is a matter of consciousness," and believed air power could effect "the adversary's consciousness significantly."[23]

Effects Based Operations proponents within the IDF came to believe that an enemy could be completely immobilized by precision air attacks against critical military systems. The Israeli supporters of EBO also hypothesized that little or no land forces would be required since it would not be necessary to destroy the enemy.[24] Surprisingly, there were also IDF officers who "did not believe that they would ever confront conventional warfare again, and as a result, they did not prepare," wrote Russell W. Glenn. Confident in their assessments, the IAF removed Close Air Support (CAS) missions from their fixed-wing pilots and detached IAF liaison officers from IDF brigade level staffs.[25]

The Chief of the IDF General Staff was also saddled with a new doctrine which he endorsed and signed into effect in April 2006. The "core of this document is the theory of SOD (Systemic Operational Design)" noted one its creators, retired Israeli Brigadier General Shimon Naveh.[26] The new design was intended as a tool to help IDF commanders plan their campaigns and contained terminology drawn from "post modern French philosophy, literary theory, architecture and psychology."[27] According to Milan N. Vego, "SOD enthusiasts claim that modern military operations are too complicated for applying a linear approach because the enemy and environment form a complex adaptive system. However, they mistakenly argue that such systems cannot be destroyed but must be pushed into disequilibrium—that is, into chaos."[28]

Naveh maintained that his design was "not intended for ordinary mortals" causing many IDF officers to perhaps wonder just how many demigods were in the IDF.[29] Clearly scores of officers were troubled by the new terminology and methodology that had worked its way into the new doctrine. Many believed that an "intellectual virus" was distorting the IDF's fundamental doctrine.[30] A former IAF fighter pilot and current reservist in the IAF Campaign Planning Department observed that the new doctrine was:

> Similar to SOD, it replaces the "old" structure of Mission, Commander's Intent, Forces and Tasks . . . with a whole new world of Political Directive, Strategic Purpose, System Boundaries, operational Boundaries, Campaign's Organizing Theme, Opposite System Rationale . . . and so on. Field commanders did not like the new doctrine, principally because they didn't understand it. Of the 170 pages long doctrine document, many experienced officers didn't understand more than half. Officers responsible for planning EBOs in the Air Force, could not understand the definition of EBO (more precisely in Hebrew Effect-Based Campaigns) or of the definition of the word "Campaign" in the document. The terminology used was too complicated, vain, and could not be understood by the thou-

sands of officers that needed to carry it out . . . The new terminology and methodology was supposed to be limited to the higher levels of command, and at the level of theater command and definitely at the division level, the old terminology and methodology should have been used. Nonetheless, it trickled down . . . Commanders need to speak in a simple accessible manner, composed essentially of two things: what do we occupy and what do we blow up. This is understandable. When an order is given to render the enemy "incoherent" or to make the enemy feel "distress" or "chased down," or to "achieve standoff domination of the theater" field commanders simply do not know what to do and cannot judge how well or how bad they are progressing.[31]

The circumstances surrounding the new IDF doctrine was muddled further by the fact that Halutz likely did not understand what he had signed. "He's an idiot," Naveh stated, "He's really a fool; he's a clown. He signed something that he really has never bothered to learn . . . What really worried me were the blind followers, and the IDF was full of them. They were just mumbling the words without really appreciating what lay in the base of these words—and Halutz was such a guy. He was just using the right words but never really bothered to understand. Understanding implies learning, and learning is painful."[32] While a few IDF officers may have been "blind followers" of the new doctrine, one perceptive onlooker reported what many within the Israeli military thought, "that the tailors were selling nonsense, that there were no new clothes, but were too embarrassed to say so out loud. They thought they were not smart enough. Until the war came and pointed at the king's [nakedness]."[33]

Even before Halutz took command, the IDF was stretched to the limit by budgetary cuts to the ground forces and the continuing demands placed on them by the Palestinian uprising.[34] To make matters worse, soldiers with perishable combat skills, such as tank crewmen, patrolled the West Bank and Gaza Strip on foot or in jeeps, in some cases going years without training on their armored vehicles. A distraught reserve armor battalion commander condemned the three IDF chiefs of staff before Halutz, "for having neglected the land forces in favor of the air force, for sacrificing ground mobility on the altar of high-tech wizardry, and for squandering tank specialists in the nooks and crannies of the intifada." He also pointed out that reservist tank crews received little training prior to the outbreak of war in the summer of 2006. "To be in top form," he stated, "a tank reservist needs a five-day refresher exercise each year. Most hardly got that in the course of three years, others in the space of five, and yet others none at all."[35] Remarkably, as the IDF prepared for war against Hezbollah, there was at least one battalion commander within its ranks who had never conducted a night movement with his unit. Further more, there were junior officers who had gone five years without participating in one combat-training exercise.[36]

The IDF also made sizable cuts in the reserve ground forces budget and equipment. According to the Winograd Report, "the quality of the equipment in the depots sent a message about values to the reserve soldiers. And in fact, missing, obsolete or broken equipment told the reservist that there was no one making sure that he would be equipped in a manner . . . that would allow him to operate in an optimal way . . . when he was called to the flag."[37]

Perhaps even more disturbing than the cuts in the reserves and the breakdown of skills at the tactical level, was the fact that many high-ranking IDF officers, both regular and reserve, had not received adequate training. "Brigade [commanders] were under-trained, and commanders above brigade level did not command their units in training for years," Tira wrote. "Some reserve units did not train in large formations for 4-6 years. What is interesting here is that this under-training was not the result of neglect or omission, but of intentional policy." Under the IDF's new doctrine, the Corps formation was eliminated, and plans were in the works to abolish the Division as well when the war erupted in 2006. According to Tira, Halutz and the followers of Naveh's SOD, "did not see a role for land formations larger than a brigade . . . The important point is that they did not see training above brigade level as important and therefore did not invest in it." Tira also concluded that the new doctrine inflated the "focus on the cognitive side of war and the media war. Instead of killing the bad guys like in the good old days, they wanted to create a 'consciousness of victory' on our side and 'cognitive perception of defeat' on the other side."[38]

In response to the kidnapping, Halutz convinced Olmert and Peretz that Israel should strike back against Hezbollah and the Lebanese central government with a substantial air campaign. The plan was not designed to directly or fully crush Hezbollah's capabilities, but to produce "effects" that would force Hezbollah out of southern Lebanon, and cause them to disarm.[39] Halutz proposed an immense air strike against "symbolic" Lebanese targets and Hezbollah's military resources. The plan also called for targeted strikes against Hezbollah's military and political leadership. "His idea," Naveh stated, "was that . . . we hit all these targets [and] Hezbollah will collapse as a military organization. No one really believed that the Lebanese government was in position to really pressure Hezbollah. The idea was that Hezbollah would give up and then everybody would go home happy. Again the idea was to change something in the equation, to change the conditions by forcing them to become political and abandon the military option."[40] Hezbollah however, had prepared for an effects based campaign, and the Lebanese government was too weak and therefore incapable of challenging Hezbollah. There was simply no lever to pull that would cause Hezbollah to crumple.[41]

The stage was now set to reveal to the world what one Israeli writer described as "a witches brew of high tech fantasies and basic unpreparedness [sic]."[42] On the night of 12 July, Israeli jets and artillery began limited attacks on infrastructure targets across Lebanon, Hezbollah's rockets, command and control centers, and its mouthpiece, al-Manar television. Just after midnight an IAF squadron flying in the vicinity of Beirut attacked and destroyed 54 Hezbollah Zelzal rocket launchers. When Halutz received word of the mission's success he informed Olmert by secure phone that "All the long-range rockets have been destroyed. We've won the war." Israel would soon learn that his declaration of mission accomplished could not have been further from the truth.[43]

The IAF's attacks on Hezbollah however, proved ineffectual. Attempts to compromise its logistical sites and defensive positions in the opening three days of the war proved futile as did a targeted attack on Hezbollah's leadership in Beirut. A US official who closely monitored the war speculated that the IAF air strikes impacted only 7% of Hezbollah's military resources.[44]

As early as 14 July, Israeli intelligence suggested to high ranking military and political leaders that air power alone could not accomplish the mission. The intelligence "concluded that the heavy bombing campaign and small ground offensive [small IDF Special Forces incursions] then underway would show 'diminishing returns' within days. It stated that the plan would neither win the release of the two Israeli soldiers in Hezbollah's hands nor reduce the militia's rocket attacks on Israel to fewer than 100 a day."[45]

It soon became clear to some within the IDF, that if Israeli war aims were to be successfully prosecuted, the IDF would probably have to launch a major ground offensive into southern Lebanon. However, as Halutz and his senior commanders mulled over the situation, alarming reports began to trickle into headquarters from small IDF Special Forces units conducting probes into southern Lebanon. They reported, "Hezbollah units were fighting tenaciously to hold their positions on the first ridgeline overlooking Israel."[46]

On 17 July, the first large scale Israeli ground foray began near Maroun al-Ras, in an effort to establish a foothold in southern Lebanon.[47] One of the first units to come to blows with Hezbollah in Maroun al-Ras was the elite Maglan unit, part of what the IDF called a "special forces cluster."[48] "We didn't know what hit us," one Maglan soldier told a reporter. The special forces soldiers were stunned by the volume of gunfire and the doggedness of the Hezbollah fighters. "We expected a tent and three Kalashnikovs—that was the intelligence we were given. Instead, we found a hydraulic steel door leading to a well-equipped network of tunnels," another Maglan reported. By the next morning, the Maglans were almost surrounded. It was reported from northern headquarters, that, "The commander of the IDF's northern sector, Lieutenant-General Udi Adams, could barely believe that some of his best soldiers had been so swiftly trapped; neither could the chief of staff. 'What's wrong with the Maglans?' Halutz demanded to know. 'They are surrounded,' Adam replied quietly. 'I must send in more forces.'"[49]

From their underground bunkers and tunnels, Hezbollah fighters in and around Maroun al-Ras fought back frantically. As the battle intensified, the IDF was forced to throw more forces into the fray. Soon, tanks from three Israeli brigades entered the fight, along with the Egoz unit from the Golani Brigade, an engineer battalion, and Battalion 101 of the Paratrooper Brigade. On 19 July, a Hezbollah anti-tank missile killed five Egoz soldiers as they sought shelter in a house.[50] At the same time, numerous IDF tanks were hit by long-range anti-tank missiles that wounded many of the tank crewmen. "They're not fighting like we thought they would," one IDF soldier said. "They're fighting harder. They're good on their own ground." In fact, Hezbollah's tactical proficiency bewildered the IDF. Hezbollah was not simply hunkering down and defending terrain but was using its small-arms, mortars, rockets, and anti-tank weapons to successfully maneuver against the IDF.[51]

Although some of the problems surrounding the IDF's performance in Maroun al-Ras remain murky, there were major criticisms voiced by both officers and soldiers concerning tactics and casualties. Early in the fight, reports circulated that growing concern over casualties caused IDF commanders to become overly cautious. Reports also confirmed a lack of combined arms expertise and a deficiency in basic tactical skills.[52] Years of counterinsurgency operations against the Palestinians had greatly eroded the IDF's conventional war fighting proficiency. An IDF general pointed out, "It's one thing to give the troops maps, target list, etc. It's another thing to be trained for the mission—they weren't trained . . ."[53]

Taken aback by the ineffective air campaign and surprised by Hezbollah's stubborn resistance in Maroun al-Ras, Olmert and Halutz called-up Israeli reserve forces on 21 July. One source concluded that, "the decision to call the reserves took key senior reserve officers, usually the first to be notified of a pending call-up, by surprise. The reserve call-up was handled chaotically—with the reserve 'tail' of logistical support lagging some 24-48 hours behind the deployment of reserve forces."[54] Contrary to the opinion of some, the call-up was not designed to assist the regular army in a massive ground invasion of southern Lebanon. Although it would allow Israel to amass forces along the border, Hulutz's ground plan would remain unchanged. There would be no determined effort to drive Hezbollah back across the Litani or destroy its rockets with a large-scale ground assault. A general on Hulutz's staff told a reporter on 22 July, that "The goal is not necessarily to eliminate every Hezbollah rocket. What we must do is disrupt the military logic of Hezbollah. I would say that this is still not a matter of days away." Many ground commanders were stunned by the remark and questioned the true aims of the war.[55]

By 5 August, the IDF had approximately 10,000 soldiers in southern Lebanon. In three weeks of war, the ground forces had managed to penetrate no further than four miles. Remarkably, the border zone was still unsecured as were the towns of Maroun al Ras and Bint Jbeil.[56] Yet the entire Hezbollah force south of the Litani consisted of only 3,000 fighters. Unlike the IDF, Hezbollah did not call on its sizable reserve forces and chose to fight the entire war south of the Litani with its original force of 3,000 men.[57] For Israel and the IDF there was still no "spectacle of victory," or any sign of Hezbollah's impending defeat.

"They are experts at deception," a soldier pointed out after weeks of battling Hezbollah. "Everyone will think they won no matter what. That's how you win when there's a few thousand of you and 50,000 of us. The more of them we kill, the more of them who are generated. Unfortunately, this is a lost war." As Hezbollah rockets continued to kill Israeli civilians, IDF ground forces continued to battle their elusive foe. Many of the IDF soldiers were amazed by Hezbollah's elaborate bunker and tunnel system. One infantryman reported finding a bunker near Maroun al-Ras "that was more than 25 feet deep and contained a network of tunnels linking several large storage rooms and multiple entrances and exits. He said it was equipped with a camera at the entrance, linked to a monitor below to help Hezbollah fighters ambush Israeli soldiers."[58]

While the IDF had some tactical successes, one senior Israeli intelligence officer remarked that Hezbollah fighters had "gone to school" on IDF ground forces and described the foe as "an infantry brigade with modern weapons."

By 8 August, 61 Israeli soldiers had been killed, while the IDF reported 450 Hezbollah fighters killed. This last figure was highly exaggerated, as it appears likely that only 184 Hezbollah fighters were killed in ground fighting in southern Lebanon during the entire war.[59]

While many within the IDF and the Israeli public remained perplexed over Halutz's effects based ground campaign of "raids" and "enter and pull-out missions," retired Israeli politicians and seasoned IDF officers became increasingly alarmed. One report stated:

> As the fighting dragged on, some veteran officers lost patience with what they saw as the inexperience of the chief of staff and defence minister. "What are you doing in Lebanon, for God's sake?" the former defence minister, General Shaul Mofaz, asked Olmert. "Why did you go into Bint Jbeil? It was a trap set by Hezbollah." Mofaz proposed an old-fashioned IDF assault plan to launch a blitzkrieg against Hezbollah, reach the strategically important Litani River in 48 hours and then demolish Hezbollah in six days. Olmert liked the idea but Peretz did not appreciate his predecessor's intervention and rejected it. Olmert appeared to lose confidence and began to issue conflicting orders. "Our mission changed twice, three times every day," complained one soldier. Many Israelis have been left furious that the legendary deterrent power of their army has been shattered.[60]

On 11 August, the UN Security Council unanimously approved Resolution 1701 which was designed to implement a cease-fire and end the war as soon as possible. A UN press release declared, "the utmost concern at the spiraling deadly violence and destruction in Lebanon," and called "for a full cessation of hostilities in the month-long war between Israel and Hezbollah, mapping out a formula for the phased withdrawal of the Israel Defence Forces from southern Lebanon, while up to 15,000 United Nations peacekeepers help Lebanese troops take control of the area."[61]

Knowing full well that the war would be over in days and the old border re-established, Olmert and Peretz made the decision to expand the war effort by ordering their divisions north to the Litani. It was perhaps one of the most bizarre episodes of the war. While the reasoning for the offensive maneuver remains clouded, the move was clearly not designed to annihilate Hezbollah. Ron Tira was certain that, "At no point was an order given to systemically and comprehensively deal with the rockets or Hezbollah."[62] It would appear that the IDF was still following Halutz's "raid" strategy, albeit this time with divisions instead of battalions and brigades.[63] Senior IDF officers would later state that the operation was designed as a "Battle of Awareness against Hezbollah." Others thought the operation was designed as "a kind of show designed to demonstrate to Hezbollah who is the Boss."[64]

On 11 August, the airborne reserve division under Eyal Eizenberg began moving north toward Dibel and Qana. Two Hezbollah anti-tank missiles hit a dwelling packed with 50 paratroopers after two of Eizenberg's companies were ordered to take up positions in houses in Dibel during daylight hours. The resulting explosion killed 9 and wounded 31 soldiers from the demolition company. By the time the official ceasefire went into effect on 14 August, Eizenberg's paratrooper division had managed to advance about one mile north of Dibel.[65] Along the coastal road, west of Eizenberg, unidentified IDF mechanized units managed to advance about one mile north of Mansuri by the time the war ended on 14 August.

Meanwhile, Brigadier General Gal Hirsch's Division 91 began their trek toward the Mediterranean coast, moving west from north of Bint Jbeil, where pockets of Hezbollah fighters still remained. The action proved chaotic, similar to his attacks on Maroun al-Ras and Bint Jbeil. An official government investigation after the war revealed a stunning lack of professionalism and competence in Division 91. The investigation concluded that commanders within the division "did not fully understand their orders," and "were not present with their troops during important battles and even failed to fulfill basic missions." The investigation also found fault "in the way tactical orders were composed, sometimes without a time element. Since the orders were not clear, they were changed, in some cases, on an hourly basis. Brigade commanders did not properly understand their missions . . . They didn't know what their goals were and how long they had to fulfill their missions." Remarkably, according to the report, "an entire battalion sat in the same location for several days without moving and when the commander finally received orders to push deeper into enemy territory he was confused and failed to fulfill the mission."[66]

Some of the problems within Division 91 were caused by Hirsch's operations orders. Instead of using the standard terms and format in writing his orders, Hirsch used the terminology and methodology from Halutz's new doctrine. Israeli Air Force campaign planner Ron Tira, who reviewed the orders after the war, wrote that, "When Division 91 gave its battle orders to its brigades, the orders were such that they were impossible to understand."[67] Not surprisingly, Division 91's drive to the Mediterranean fell far short of the mark by war's end.

Northeast of Division 91, Brigadier General Guy Tzur's Division 162 began its drive west from Metulla toward Qantara and Ghandouriyeh. Situated on the high-ground over looking the Litani, with east-west and north-south roads running through it, Tzur's Division saw Ghandouriyeh as a key piece of terrain. For over a week Tsur had planned to capture the town, but each time his division initiated the orders, higher headquarters abruptly canceled them.

In an effort to provide cover for the tanks and clear the high ground above the Saluki Wadi, Division 162 air-assaulted in elements of the Nahal Infantry Brigade. The soldiers apparently landed unopposed on the outskirts of Farun and Ghandouriyeh. It is likely that the soldiers of the Nahal Brigade occupied several buildings in the three Lebanese towns and did little in the way of clearing the high ground above the Wadi. On 12 August, however, they informed their commander that the area was secure.[68]

With the high ground presumably secure, 24 tanks of Brigade 401 began crossing the Wadi Saluki. Soon after moving forward, the two lead tanks in the column found their route blocked by a collapsed building. As the tanks searched for another crossing point, a large IED or mine exploded behind them, collapsing the road. At precisely the same moment, a Hezbollah Kornet laser guided anti-tank missile slammed into a company commander's Merkava, killing him and the entire crew. Within seconds, swarms of anti-tank missiles assailed the tank column. Amazingly, the IDF reported that not a single tank crew in the Wadi used the smokescreen system on their tanks to help protect them from the fusillade of deadly missiles.[69] One of the ambushed tank crewmen recalled that "When the first tank was hit, we knew that the nightmare had begun. You should understand that the first missile which hits is not the really dangerous missile. The ones which come afterward are the dangerous ones—and there always follow four or five after the first . . . It was hellfire, and have no idea when it will get you. You just pray that it will end at last, that the volley will end and that you will hear on the radio that everybody is OK. But, unfortunately, that is not what we heard when the shooting ended, no sir!"[70]

Pinned down by Hezbollah anti-tank missiles, direct fire weapons, and mortars, the infantry soldiers of the Nahal Brigade were hard pressed to lend support to the tank column.[71] "We thought that we were entering the Saluki after the area had been cleaned up, but then the terrorists came out of the houses and hiding places and started shooting at us as if we in a shooting range," another tank crewman remembered.[72] Incredibly, there was no coordination whatsoever between the infantry and the tanks, and frantic calls from the trapped tank command for artillery and air support were denied by Northern Command due to concerns over fratricide.[73]

By the time the ambush ended, 11 of the 24 Merkava Mark 4 tanks in Wadi Saluki had been hit by anti-tank missiles.[74] Eight tank crewmen and four infantrymen were killed. Although the exact number of wounded is not yet established, both the battalion commander and his deputy in the tank column were wounded.[75] It would appear that by the time the cease-fire went into effect, Division 162 had advanced no further than Ghandouriyeh. An officer from Division 162 stated that, "There were many professional mistakes made in the use of the tanks. The soldiers were not trained properly for this battle and the division lacked experience in using tanks and infantry units operating together and in this type of terrain."[76] Undoubtedly, the actions of Division 162 at Wadi Saluki, underscore the dismal state of the IDF's ground forces, particularity in conducting conventional maneuver operations.

To the north of Tzur's Division 162, Brigadier General Erez Zuckerman's reserve armored division was also having difficulty implementing the so-called "Battle of Awareness." While the operations of the reserve armored division remains sketchy, there appears to have been major problems within the command. Zuckerman was "castigated" by an official IDF investigative team after the war for the poor performance of his tank units. The report also stated that "his lack of training led to many failures."[77] Zuckerman would later relinquish his command, telling his superiors that "I have failed and I resign . . . Toward the end of the war I felt that I had failed in my duty and decided to take personal responsibility . . . I told this to my commanders and subordinates every chance I got."[78] According to an Israeli source, out of 11 IDF brigade commanders only one ever crossed the border into Lebanon by wars end.[79]

On 13 August, one day before the cease-fire, the IDF conducted air-assaults and airborne drops south the Litani. These air assaults and airborne drops were intended to expand Israeli control to the Latani. This decision could easily have had calamitous results if not for the implementation of the cease-fire. According to one source, most of the IDF soldiers were "immediately surrounded" once they hit the ground. Although many regarded the decision as purely political, one retired IDF officer went so far as to assert that Olmert was "using the military for public relations purposes."[80]

Halutz monitored these last missions from inside his bunker in Tel Aviv. When he received word that one of the IDF's Sikorsky CH-53 helicopters had been shot down by Hezbollah, killing the entire crew, the chief of staff purportedly exclaimed that he "felt defeated, both personally and professionally." Hezbollah, in a final act of defiance, fired 250 rockets into Israel in the closing hours before the cease-fire.[81]

"Training, Training and Training As Well As Innovative Thinking": The IDF Response to the 2006 War With Hezbollah

The Israeli government's response to the dismal performance of the IDF during the 2006 Hezbollah-Israeli war was swift and revealing. In short order, Prime Minister Ehud Olmert's government formed a committee to investigate problems associated with the conflict. The Winograd Report findings severely criticized Olmert, Defense Minister Peretz and Chief of the IDF General Staff, Halutz. The report also concluded that the IDF had not been ready for war. In one of its more pointed barbs, the report concluded that, "All in all, the IDF failed, especially because of the conduct of the high command and the ground forces, to provide an effective military response to the challenge posed to it by the war in Lebanon, and thus failed to provide the political echelon with a military achievement that could have served as a basis for political and diplomatic action. Responsibility for this outcome lies mainly with the IDF, but the misfits between the mode of action and the goals determined by the political echelon share responsibility."[82]

Both Peretz and Halutz resigned by the summer of 2007.[83] According to Russell W. Glenn, "a considerable number of Israelis blame the poor performance during the 2006 war, in part, on their prime minister and defense minister lacking requisite military experience."[84] Indeed, many Israelis did believe that proven combat leaders were required at the helm. Peretz was soon replaced by Former Prime Minister Ehud Barak. In terms of military experience, there could not have been a greater contrast between the two men. While Peretz had fulfilled his military obligation as a maintenance officer in the IDF, Barak was a highly decorated combat veteran and a former special forces leader as well as commander of a Tank Brigade and Armored Division. Furthermore, Barak had also commanded a tank battalion in the Sinai during the 1973 Yom Kippur War and in 1991 was promoted to Lieutenant General, thereby becoming the 14th Chief of the General Staff.[85]

Halutz's replacement, Lieutenant General Gabi Ashkenazi, was also a solid IDF combat veteran.[86] Ashkenazi had fought in the Yom Kippur war, participated in the Entebbe Operation in 1976 and was the former commander of the Golani Brigade, as well as a former IDF Deputy Chief of Staff. Both Halutz and Ashkenazi were in the running for the position of Chief of the General Staff in 2005. When Halutz won the coveted appointment, Ashkenazi abruptly resigned. After two years as a civilian however, Ashkenazi returned to active duty, determined, as one IDF official put it, "to pull the IDF out of the muck."[87]

To his credit, Halutz instituted at series of 70 fact-finding teams before his departure. Twenty of these teams focused directly or indirectly on the General Staff, while others focused almost exclusively on issues connected with IDF operations in the field. Once in command, Ashkenazi appointed his own team of high-ranking officers to study the findings of the Winograd Report, weighing it against the IDF's own internal probe. According to one source, "The IDF has made sure it has all the answers needed to rebut whatever arguments [a]rose regarding the military, thus attempting to send the message that the military had already identified all the major failures during its own probe of the war, implementing the lessons learnt accordingly." Indeed, by September 2007, Ashkenazi introduced "Teffen 2012," a five year plan meant to increase the war fighting ability of the IDF. One of the major goals of "Teffen 2012" was to create "A decisive ground maneuver capability based on modern main battle tanks (MBTs) and other armored fighting vehicles, attack helicopters, low altitude unmanned aerial vehicles (UAVs) and transport aircraft." The plan also envisioned advancements in "precision strike capability" by the IAF, as well as, "intelligence superiority through all means of gathering" and "preparedness and sustainability through expanding emergency stocks of munitions."[88] Senior officers were also quick to point out that a number of the adjustments made by the IDF after the 2006 war "were not short of 'revolutionary,' but admitted that the military would not be able to objectively assess their efficiency until the next large operation."[89]

While some of the changes within the IDF were considered ground-breaking most simply involved a return to erstwhile military principles. "Training, training and training as well as innovative thinking," is how one officer described the IDF's response to the 2006 conflict.[90] To be sure, Ashkenazi and Barak wasted little time in implementing a sweeping transformation within the IDF.

One of the first items on the agenda was the incoherent doctrine which several of Halutz's fact finding teams had already "branded" as "completely wrong." These teams concluded that the doctrine used during the 2006 campaign created "confusion in terminology and misunderstanding of basic military principles." Long-established IDF modus operandi had been replaced by "an alternative 'conceptual framework' for military thinking, replacing traditional notions of 'objective' and 'subjection' with new concepts like 'campaign rational' and 'conscious-burning' of the enemy . . . Based on this doctrine, the IDF was to rely on precise stand-off fire, mostly from the air, using ground maneuvers only as a last resort."[91]

Predictably, elements related to SOD were quickly jettisoned. "SOD cancelled," was one officer's straightforward reply when questioned about changes made to IDF doctrine after 2006.[92] Using John Ellis' work *Against Deconstruction* as a backdrop to describe the failings of SOD, Yehuda Wegman, writes "that what was achieved was not a more intelligent logic, but the image of intelligence and complexity; any task undertaken made use of rhetorical means in order to create the illusion of intelligent analysis at a time when there was no such analysis." Wegman also stated that "The first casualty of the new language was the main principle of war; adhering to the mission."[93] The IDF's transient embrace of these post-modern theories at the expense of traditional principles of war is, arguably, one of the strangest episodes in the history of military doctrine.

Having abandoned SOD, the IDF went to work on a new doctrine, which has yet to be finalized. As a stopgap measure, the Israeli military has apparently returned to the doctrine in place prior to 2006.[94] Drastic changes within the IDF continued under Ashkenazi and Barak. "There was an almost immediate adjustment in training," one expert in the field acknowledged. "The IDF started training more on offensive and defensive, what we call conventional warfare skills."[95] Indeed, within the IDF Armored Corps the changes in training were swift. Tank units once again focused on their traditional roles and advantages, that of "speed and firepower." Israeli armored brigades trained for months at the IDF Ground Forces Training Center in Negev, Israel. As an example, Armored Brigade 401 that had lost eight tank crewmen during the battle of Saluki in 2006, conducted a 12-week training exercise in which they trained in urban combat, but spent most of their time "sharpening the skills needed for armored combat," according to the *Jerusalem Post*. "Our advantage is our ability to move fast and our firepower," a brigade commander emphasized. "The tanks are now driving faster and using smokescreens—something they didn't use during the war—since we now understand that the threat of anti-tank missiles is 360 degrees."[96] At the company and battalion levels, IDF units also conducted extensive and realistic training in an area meant to replicate southern Lebanon and Hezbollah tactics.[97]

The IDF reserve forces, particularly tank and artillery soldiers, were reattached to their designated weapons systems and retrained on the basics. More importantly, the reserve forces started to receive their "full equipment," stated one source, "correcting the situation of reservists who are meant to fight side by side with regular army soldiers." In the immediate aftermath of the 2006 war, the IDF procured "10,000 ceramic protection vests; 30,000 helmets; 40,000 combat vests" and "60,000 night vision goggles," as well as significant quantities of grenades, small arms ammunition and magazines. After years of performing "other" duties the reserve soldiers returned to their equipment to address what one observer called "classic warfare needs."[98]

With a new lengthened training program in place, the reserve armored corps began conducting live fire exercises and participating in full scale division maneuver training. These exercises included both combat forces and combat support units. Unlike 2006, when some reserve officers never met many of their soldiers, these large exercises, for the first time in years, brought everyone in the organization together. Furthermore, all reserve officers selected for command were sent to the proper schools and directed to conduct regular exercises with all forces under their command.[99] It was also suggested that the IDF reserve create a new "fitness index" resembling the one used by the IAF to qualify pilots.[100]

By late 2008, the IDF had undergone an almost complete transformation. Having scrutinize and examined its missteps during the 2006 war with Hezbollah, the IDF abandoned the defective doctrine of the past and returned to the fundamentals of modern warfare. If airpower and precision fires were to be decisive, they must be coupled with well trained and highly motivated combined arms ground maneuver forces. Air power alone could never be the sole harbinger of victory. As the IDF continued to train, Hamas rockets started to rain down on Israel from Gaza. This time, the IDF would be prepared.

The Gaza Conflict

After winning local elections against its political rival, Fatah, in 2006, Hamas gained complete control of Gaza in 2007, by forcibly confronting the Palestinian Authority and driving them out of the region. These actions were carried out by the Izz al-Din al Qassam Brigades, the military wing of Hamas. By 2008 the force had grown to approximately 15,000 fighters and was considered the "most organized and effective militia in the Palestinian Territories."[101] As Anthony H. Cordesman reported however, their triumph over Fatah, "occurred far more because of a lack of leadership and elementary competence on the part of the Fatah/Palestinian Authority Forces than any great skill on the part of Hamas. Unlike the Hezbollah, Hamas never had to develop the combat skills necessary to fight an effective opponent."[102]

Israel responded to Hamas' actions by establishing an economic blockade. According to Cordesman, "some 1.5 million Palestinians in Gaza became hostages to the power struggle between Israel and Hamas." As the noose tightened, Hamas responded by smuggling in weaponry, much of which was supplied by Iran and Syria. Small arms, rocket propelled grenades, mortars and rockets were funneled through tunnel systems connecting Egypt and Gaza, and through the Sinai and the Mediterranean Sea. From time to time Hamas used its rockets and mortars to attack Israel, to which the IDF responded in kind.

Hamas attempted to replicate a Hezbollah type defensive system in preparation for any IDF incursion into Gaza. Cordesman was convinced that Hamas attempted to follow the pattern established by Hezbollah in an effort to "create tunnels and strong points in Gaza, develop new booby traps and improvised explosive devices (IEDs), and to create [a] spider web of prepared strong points, underground and hidden shelters, and ambush points throughout urban and built up areas as defensive strong points."[103]

An Israeli military source described Gaza as "one big minefield, IEDs, traps and tunnels in almost every block."[104] Hamas was also fully prepared to use the civilian population as human shields and to fire rockets from mosques, schools and hospitals. They were also not opposed to placing weapons and rocket stockpiles in civilian homes and to fight a "war amongst the people." Hamas would attempt to counter Israel's massive firepower by placing its fighters in the midst of the population. According to one source, "Kill zones" were to be "set up with no regard for the consequences for non-combatants."[105] To prevail, Hamas would have to tie down the IDF in a vicious urban fight while it attempted to triumph on the world stage through the clever manipulation of the media.[106]

While endeavoring to replicate Hezbollah's tactics might have seemed a good idea, there were several major factors that would prove highly problematic for Hamas. The first issue was that Hamas lacked the training and fighting prowess of Hezbollah. One IDF officer explained that Hamas was not as well trained as Hezbollah and not as "highly motivated." However, he continued, Hamas is "an organized force, trained and equipped by Iran. If Hezbollah is the Delta Force, then Hamas is the National Guard."[107] Unlike Hezbollah in 2006, Hamas also lacked large quantities of sophisticated antitank missiles without which they would be hard pressed to stop IDF tanks.[108] Secondly, the rugged terrain in southern Lebanon was ideal for defensive operations, while Gaza was much smaller area, as well as flat and heavily urbanized. According to an Israeli military source, it represented a "completely different war DNA."[109]

After months of continued small scale back and forth skirmishing, a bilateral ceasefire was agreed to by Hamas and Israel on 19 June 2008. Not designed to foster a lasting peace, the break from fighting simply allowed both sides to prepare for the next round of hostilities. Hamas used the time to continue work on its defenses and to smuggle more weapons into Gaza, including 122-mm, Grad and Improved Grad rockets from Iran. Meanwhile in Israel, the IDF began planning its response.

Unlike 2006, in which Israel had no time to design a coherent response to Hezbollah, the IDF began covertly preparing a masterful campaign plan against Hamas. "These plans," wrote Cordesman, "included an air attack phase, an air-ground phase to further weaken Hamas and secure areas in the north, and a contingency plan to seal off the Philadelphia Corridor and the Gazan-Egyptian border. All who were asked specifically stated that the IDF did not go to war with plans to conduct a sustained occupation, to try to destroy Hamas or all its forces, or to reintroduce the Palestinian Authority and Fatah, although such contingency plans and exercises may have existed."[110]

With ample time to prepare, the IDF was also able to collect an unprecedented amount of highly sensitive information on Hamas, enabling it to gain complete intelligence domination. In fact, Israel had been preparing a "mosaic" of Hamas targets for years. The lull created by the ceasefire provided an opportunity to combine this information with recently obtained Human Intelligence (HUMINT). This created "a remarkably accurate picture of Hamas targets in Gaza that it constantly updated on a near real time basis," wrote Cordesman. The IDF and Israeli intelligence networks (Shin Bet) completely "penetrated" Hamas' network at all levels.[111] More than one IDF commander commented that they had been "blind in Lebanon, but in Gaza they could see everything . . . the operations in Gaza were 200% better."[112]

In early November 2008, the IDF launched a raid that killed six Hamas fighters inside the Gaza Strip. Hamas responded with a torrent of rockets fired into Israel and announced it would end the ceasefire on 18 December 2008. This would prove a costly blunder for Hamas as it clearly alerted Israel of its intentions, method and date. Unlike Hezbollah which was thoroughly prepared for war in 2006, Hamas was unprepared to do battle with the IDF in the closing days of 2008. The Izz al-Din al Qassam Brigades had yet to complete their tunnel systems or established a new secure communications network. They were also lagging behind in planning for logistical operations, as well as the deployment of certain weapons systems.[113]

Between 4 November and 21 December, Hamas fired a total of 200 rockets into Israel. As the month of December drew to a close, Hamas continued to taunt the Israelis with ongoing rocket and mortar fire. Like Hezbollah in 2006, Hamas had greatly underestimated the eventual Israeli response.[114]

After implementing a highly detailed deception plan, which convinced Hamas that it had no plans to engage in a full scale conflict, the IDF launched Operation CAST LEAD. At 1130 on 27 December, IAF aircraft roaring in from the Mediterranean struck numerous Hamas targets in an expansive assault that was the largest ever carried out in Gaza. In the first passes 180 Hamas targets were hit. Weapon storage facilities, rocket assembly plants, Hamas training camps, command centers, communication networks and other targets were destroyed with masterful precision.[115]

As the IAF precision munitions continued to rain down, Hamas fighters managed to fire approximately 50 rockets into Israel, killing one civilian and wounding six others. As Hamas firing squads scurried to launch their rockets and mortars however, they were met by a hail of fire from both IDF fixed wing aircraft and attack helicopters. "Virtually all IAF fixed wing strikes," wrote Cordesman, "could be carried out from aircraft fully loaded with their maximum payload of precision weapons, and which could carry out multiple strikes per sorties on relatively soft targets." On the first day alone, approximately 200 Palestinians were killed, the vast majority of whom were Hamas fighters. The IAF proudly announced that, "The targets had been marked by intelligence collected during the months preceding the attack."[116]

For the next several days the IDF continued to pummel Hamas from the air. The Israeli Navy also moved in off the coast of Gaza, striking numerous Hamas targets. These attacks did not however, stop all of Hamas' rockets or mortars. On 28 December, Hamas was able to launch 14 rockets and fire 16 mortar rounds into Israel. Several of the rockets landed in Gan Yavne and Bnei Darom, injuring at least five Israelis. The next day, Hamas managed to increase the number of rockets fired into Israel and launched longer range rockets into Ashdod and Ofakim. Although Israeli civilians continued to be killed and wounded, the population as a whole weathered this adversity better than in 2006.[117]

By 30 December, the IAF was convinced that they had administered "critical damage to Hamas." So great was the damage inflicted on the enemy that one IDF officer went so far as to suggest that "the IAF began its attacks at 11:30 and could have ended them at 11:40." Thus far the air campaign had been so successful that some within the IDF were equating it with the 1967 war. However, while the air missions were certainly effective, Hamas rockets and mortars continued to strike Israel.[118]

There can be little doubt that the initial air attacks against Hamas were highly successful and succeeded in knocking out many key targets as well as important Hamas commanders. Nevertheless, up until this time, as Cordesman pointed out, "Israel had not demonstrated that its ground forces, and air-land capabilities, had overcome the problems and limitations they had revealed during the fighting in Lebanon or demonstrated that they had either defeated Hamas's forces or forced it to accept any meaningful ceasefire. The IAF might have achieved most of its tactical objectives in attacking its prewar target base, but it did not achieve any major strategic or grand strategic objective."

While there were apparently some intense debates between Prime Minister Olmert and Defense Minister Barak over how the war should be conducted and when it should end, the IDF managed to stick to its campaign plan, and on 3 January 2009, released the following communiqué:[119]

Second Stage of Operation Cast Lead Begins

A short while ago IDF forces began to implement the second stage of Operation Cast Lead. Land forces have begun to maneuver within the Gaza Strip.

The objective of this stage is to destroy the terrorist infrastructure of the Hamas in the area of operation, while taking control of some of [the] rocket launching area used by the Hamas, in order to greatly reduce the quantity of rockets fired at Israel and Israeli civilians.

The IDF spokesperson emphasizes that this stage of the operation will further the goals of Operation Cast Lead as communicated till now: To strike a direct and hard blow against the Hamas while increasing the deterrent strength of the IDF, in order to bring about an improved and more stable security situation for residents of Southern Israel over the long term.

Large numbers of forces are taking part in this stage of the operation including infantry, tanks, engineering forces, artillery and intelligence with the support of the Israel Air Force, Israel navy, Israel Security Agency and other security agencies.

The operation is in accord with the decisions of the Security Cabinet. This stage of the operation is a part of the IDF's overall operational plan, and will continue on the basis of ongoing situational assessments by the IDF General Staff.

The forces participating in the operation have been highly trained and were prepared for the mission over the long period that the operation was planned. The Commander of the operation is Major General Yoav Galant, GOC Southern Command.

The IDF and the Homefront Command have taken the necessary steps to protect the civilian population. All residents of Southern Israel are requested to follow the directives of the Homefront command as communicated via the media.

The IDF spokesperson wishes to reiterate that the residents of Gaza are not the target of the operation. Those who use civilians, the elderly, women and children as "human shields" are responsible for any and all injury to the civilian population. Anyone who hides a terrorist or weapons in his house is considered a terrorist.

On the basis of a situation analysis, The IDF is taking steps to raise the level of alert for its forces in other areas of the country.[120]

The IDF launched the "second stage" or Air-Land Phase of its campaign plan on 3 January 2009. While the plan contained several alternatives for the use of ground forces in Gaza, the salient objectives were to "set tangible and achievable goals: reinforcing deterrence, weakening Hamas, [and] sharply reducing or ending the threat from smugglers and rockets over time." The blueprint also endeavored to restrict this phase to less than 10 days. "It did so," wrote Cordesman, "because it calculated that the war would begin to reach a point where serious negative consequences began to build up after about two weeks from the beginning of the first air strikes." Some of these costs included increased IDF casualties, regional instability and the steady acceleration of civilian casualties.[121] It was certainly a complete reversal from the confused, haphazard IDF response to Hezbollah. This time, the Israeli military was prepared to move forward with a well conceived plan and predetermined objectives. Unlike 2006, they would do so with a suitably trained, highly motivated ground fighting force.

During the last days of December 2008, the "Gaza Division" under the direction of Southern Command, began moving its units into fighting positions along the border. The Gaza Division was a regional or territorial division with few organic units assigned to it.[122] The division's headquarters elements were highly practiced in Gaza operations and experts on the terrain and possible combat scenarios. In the event of a ground incursion into Gaza, combat brigades from other divisions would be assigned to the Gaza Division.[123] For this operation, The Paratroopers Brigade, the Givati Brigade and the Golani Brigade were all attached to the Gaza Division. Although these brigades were under the command of the Gaza Division, they would, in fact, operate more like independent brigade task forces complete with their own artillery. Several IDF reserve brigades would also eventually come under the operational control of the Gaza Division.[124] Although "tens of thousands" of IDF reserves were called up, they would only see limited action during the closing days of the conflict.[125] Interestingly, in 2006, the IDF employed five divisions against a mere 3,000 or so Hezbollah frontline fighters; now, in Gaza, the IDF was preparing to grapple with approximately 15,000 Hamas operatives with slightly more than one division.

The IAF assigned a Forward Air Operations (FAO) officer to each brigade, giving the brigade commander "practical control" of air operations. According to Cordesman, "each brigade had its own attack helicopters and unmanned aerial vehicles, as well as on-call strike aircraft."[126] This was an important transformation considering fixed-wing CAS had been removed from the obligation to support ground forces prior to 2006. One IAF officer described the new air-land cooperation as "groundbreaking." He insisted that the "concentration of air assets in a tiny territory permitted unparalleled air-land coordination. These included UAVs clearing around corners for infantry platoons, Apaches helicopter gunships providing integral suppressive fire during movements by small units, jet fighters employed to remove mines and IEDs and to prepare the terrain for ground movements, as well as overwhelming firepower ahead of ground advances, servicing even the smallest unit."[127] To be sure, in Gaza, the IDF would use a cornucopia of innovative tactics, techniques and procedures.

The ground attack into Gaza was preceded by a massive artillery bombardment up and down the border line, which knocked out many of Hamas' defensive positions. In the north, along the coast, The Paratroopers Brigade moved south toward Atatra, while the Golani Brigade attacked from the northwest in a three-pronged advance south toward Beit Lahiya, Jabaliya and Shajaiyeh. Moving northeast from the south, the Givati Brigade advanced toward Zeitoun, while a large tank force assembled near Netzarim Junction. On the heels of the artillery salvos, the IDF forces pushed across the border, led, in most cases, by armored bulldozers. Roving above the onrushing armored columns were attack helicopters and UAVs which projected real-time intelligence back to IDF command posts. According to sources familiar with the campaign, "advanced digital systems were available at every major level of combat," and "the IDF fought with greatly improved plasma displays and ergonomic, operator friendly software." Instead of following road networks that were almost certainly mined and set for deliberate ambushes, the IDF used its armored bulldozers to smash through buildings and create alternate routes.[128]

Swarms of infantry, accompanied by bomb sniffing dogs, were used in built up areas to protect tanks and other armored vehicles from hidden explosive devises. Most, if not all of these operations were performed during hours of darkness, taking full advantage of the Hamas' lack of night fighting skills and equipment. As the Israelis pushed across the border, senior commanders advanced with them.[129] "What you are seeing today," Retired Israeli IAF General Isaac Ben Israel told the press, "is a direct lesson of what went wrong in 2006. In Lebanon we learned that if you want to stop these rockets launchers you need to send soldiers in and take the area and control it and this is what is being done now."[130]

Unlike Hezbollah, which fought tenaciously for every inch of ground in 2006, Hamas' fighters apparently had little appetite for the IDF's violent, well executed onslaught. As IDF armored vehicles roared across the border, Hamas' IEDs and roadside explosives had little to no effect. Having learned its lessons against Hezbollah, the IDF reinforced its armored vehicles to better withstand enemy IEDs and mines. Conversely, Hamas' domestically produced roadside bombs seemed to lack the explosive power of similar Hezbollah devices. As IDF ground forces advanced, Hamas' combat leaders found themselves cut off from their frontline fighters, unable to communicate or exert effective command in control.[131] "Hamas fighting prowess hardly inspired awe" an embedded Israeli journalist reported. "Hamas gunmen—in full view of the people of Gaza—abandoned the arena and fled into the crowded neighborhoods where they quickly shed their uniforms. The offensive array of bunkers and tunnels and booby-trapped buildings—set for remote detonation—were captured intact."[132]

Though most of the specific movements of IDF brigades remain classified, it is clear that the ground forces made rapid progress. Gaza City was quickly cut off from the rest of the territory. "By the third day of the air-land phase," Cordesman wrote, "the IDF was able to move forward to the point where it could begin to attack Hamas forces in detail. These operations continued to be conducted at the brigade level, rather than at the division level as in the past. This gave the forward commander much more freedom of initiative, particularly from second guessing that had sometimes reflect[ed] more concern over risk of casualties than rapid, decisive action."[133]

While this command arrangement seems to have worked, it has been suggested by some within the IDF that there was a certain "vagueness" between the political levels and the military as to objectives and end states as well as an indifference to the IDF's strategic and operational processes. "It seems," wrote an IDF officer, "as if the ministry of defense and the Chief of Staff were directly working with colonels in the field and bypassing the chain of headquarters." He maintained that this may have led to a "less effective operational design," but had, "nonetheless, to a degree succeeded." This same officer was also uncertain of whether "a clear operational design" was in place for the duration of the air-ground campaign. It was instead just "general pressure and attrition across the field," he surmised.[134]

By 5 January severe ground combat continued to flare up across Gaza, but this kind of persistent fighting was limited due to Hamas' efforts to avoid pitched battles at all cost. "In contrast," Cordesman wrote, "the IAF kept up a steady round of attacks, as did the Israeli artillery. This kept Hamas under constant pressure even when they did not engage in direct combat." When these head to head clashes did erupt however, they were often brutal. On this day, in an intense firefight between Hamas and members of the Golani Brigade, three soldiers were killed and another 24 wounded when an IDF tank mistakenly fired into a building they were occupying. What all these soldiers were doing in the same building is not known, but similar incidents transpired in 2006.[135]

Between 6-10 January, the IDF continued to put pressure on Hamas, with the IAF hitting approximately 250 targets in Gaza. The targets included Hamas rocket launching squads, rocket launching areas, smuggling tunnels, manufacture and storage facilities, sites containing hidden mortar shells, and the homes of Hamas fighters which were being used as weapons storage facilities. Groups of armed gunmen and Hamas command centers and buildings were also targeted. Israeli intelligence continued to perform well by pinpointing known Islamic Jihad fighters for the IDF. On 8 January, with the help of the Israeli intelligence the IDF killed four operatives who just days before had fired rockets into Israel.[136]

As the ground campaign continued, the IDF killed or captured hundreds of fighters and expanded its control over more and more of Gaza. Hamas' leadership was also confronted by attacks from their political rivals. To make matters even worse, they were almost entirely cut off from their fighters in the field, making command and control efforts nearly impossible.[137] Although threatened with a crushing defeat, Hamas still believed they could strengthen their standing in the Arab world by continuing to resist and conducting an effective IO campaign. However, while Hamas' propaganda machine tried to capture worldwide sympathy for their plight and paint Israel as the aggressor, the IDF pushed on relentlessly, seemingly unconcerned about any wide-reaching IO effort. One IDF officer was convinced that the Israelis would never win global public opinion, but thought their IO campaign had worked well in conveying the message that, "we did as we pleased, when we pleased, and where we pleased—full battle space domination." He also considered the IDF's ability to be "less transparent" in this conflict as a positive factor.[138]

To the IDF's credit, legal planners fully participated in the development of operation CAST LEAD and great pains were taken to limit civilian casualties. In fact, the IDF set up call centers with Arabic speakers to call homes that were targeted for destruction, giving the occupants a reasonable amount of time to evacuate the premises. According to one source the call center was under stringent orders to convey the message to adults only. Nevertheless, many Palestinian civilians were killed or wounded and Hamas took full advantage of the situation to increase its popular standing on the world stage.[139]

From 8 to 18 January, the IDF continued to batter Hamas with its air-land capabilities. Soldiers from the Givati Brigade would later tell the press that they had put into service many of the lessons learned from the 2006 campaign against Hezbollah. Officers from the brigade spoke in glowing terms of their new fighting principles "such as commitment to mission and pushing for contact with the enemy." Indeed, a fresh, innovative spirit seemed to radiate from many IDF ground units. A battalion commander in the Givati Brigade stated during the height of the ground battle that his men "must deal with the enemy and nothing else. We are focusing on the mission. We haven't even received newspapers here. When we finish what we have been tasked with, we'll express interest in what people up there are saying about it." Cell phones were also removed from IDF soldiers so they could focus more intently on the battle and not the home front, and to thwart any problems with Communications Security (COMSEC).[140]

On 11 January, after what one Israeli officer called a bit of "fine-tuning," IDF reserve forces began moving into Gaza. Under the command of the Gaza Division, the reserve brigades moved into the sectors already secured by regular IDF forces, allowing the regular infantry to continue offensive operations. In the two weeks prior to their commitment into Gaza, the reserve brigades trained intensely at the Ground Training Center in Tze'elim. "New and advanced equipment was issued to the reservist," the IDF reported, "and they have expressed their satisfaction about the quality of the equipment and emphasized its role in the improvement of their operational abilities." To be sure, the training provided, as well as the upgrading of equipment, helped produce a force far superior to the IDF reserves employed against Hezbollah in 2006.[141]

As the reserve brigades rolled into Gaza, the IDF air-ground campaign continued to kill and capture Hamas fighters. On 13 January, the IDF reported that they had already captured hundreds of Hamas gunmen while the Givati and Paratroopers Brigades continued to destroy weapons stores and tunnels. Together, the ground forces and the IAF were also able to eradicate 22 cells of Hamas fighters in synchronized operations. While the IAF also managed to knockout 20 rocket launching sites, Hamas was nonetheless able to launch 2 rockets and fire 12 mortar rounds into Israel. Since the opening of hostilities, Hamas indirect fire had killed 3 Israeli civilians and wounded 255 others.[142]

While the IDF still listed its main objectives as "the creation of a better security situation . . . cessation of rocket and mortar fire and all terrorist attacks from the Gaza Strip," the situation was rapidly reaching a decision point. The IDF could either expand the ground campaign significantly in an effort to eradicate all rockets, mortars and Hamas fighters, or Israel could begin to move toward a ceasefire. Expanding the campaign could have resulted in increased casualties for the IDF and Israeli and Palestinian civilians. Palestinian civilian casualties and the massive destruction produced by the conflict were already causing mounting apprehension around the world. As Cordesman pointed out, "The air-land phase of the fighting scored continuing tactical gains, but it also exacerbated the political, strategic, and humanitarian problems that had arisen during the air phase." On 13 January a senior IDF officer informed the press that the "political echelon will have to make [a] decision on [the] military operation's future."[143] After five more days of fighting, the Israeli cabinet announced a unilateral ceasefire in Gaza on 18 January.

Conclusion

The IDF's campaign against Hamas undoubtedly proved an impressive achievement. While the enemy the Israeli military confronted certainly lacked many of the traits normally associated with a professional fighting force and indubitably fell far short of the combat prowess of Hezbollah, these facts do not diminish the IDF's accomplishments. In the end, the IDF's real triumph was not its ability to quash an inferior military organization like Hamas, but how the Israeli military retrained and restructured its ground forces in the wake of their disappointing performance in 2006. These post war re-examinations and alterations allowed it to defeat Hamas so decisively and convincingly that would-be enemies of Israel could not fail to take note.

There were striking differences between the 2006 war with Hezbollah and the recent conflict with Hamas. The peculiar doctrine in place in 2006, which ran counter to the basic principles of war, was abandoned in favor of more classic military principles. These included mission and aim, initiative and offensive, continuity of action and the maintenance of morale and fighting spirit. All of these principles were absent in southern Lebanon, but on full display in Gaza. The incomprehensible SOD elements were replaced and the IDF returned to a policy of commitment to the mission and more importantly, simplicity.[144]

There was also a vast difference in leadership during the course of the two conflicts. Defense Minister Peretz, a man with no combat experience, was replaced by Ehud Barak, a solid leader and ground combat veteran. By 2008, the verbose Halutz had been replaced by the veteran no-nonsense ground commander Ashkenazi. While Halutz was prone to wordy, garrulous public statements during the 2006 war, Ashkenazi remained relatively silent during the Gaza campaign. Even as Barak and Prime Minister Olmert were rumored to have argued over the direction and time table of the Gaza operation, Ashkenazi managed to adhere to the IDF's campaign plan. It was indeed a far cry from Halutz's ever-changing approach in 2006.

Another major difference between 2006 and the Gaza campaign was training and equipment. In 2006, IDF ground forces, both regulars and reserves, were for the most part untaught and ill-equipped for a war against Hezbollah. Senior officers and enlisted soldiers alike floundered in southern Lebanon. Lacking basic war fighting skills, and in many cases basic combat equipment, they proved no match for Hezbollah. Both tankers and artillerymen had for too long been separated from their equipment, causing competence and proficiency to suffer.

Owing to the hard work and foresight of Barak and Ashkenazi, the IDF's situation had changed dramatically by 2008. In Gaza, senior officers, leading from the front, understood their responsibilities and were able to maneuver their forces. Soldiers were trained not only in basic combat skills, but were proficient in the use of their equipment. In Gaza, soldiers were fully trained and equipped for night fighting and were highly proficient in indirect fire skills. More importantly, the IDF, in a short space of time, was able to regain its combined arms maneuver capabilities.

The 2006 Hezbollah-Israeli war and the recent clash in Gaza demonstrate that even a historically successful army can be caught unprepared by a resourceful, imaginative enemy. The IDF proved adept at indentifying and analyzing its mistakes and miscalculations. A rigorous training program that focused on time honored principles of warfare enabled the IDF to restore competence and credibility in its ground forces. One needs to look no further than the recent Gaza conflict to affirm its success in this endeavor.

NOTES

1. Ian Black, "Six months of Secret Planning—Then Israel Moves Against Hamas," *The Guardian*, 29 December 2008.

2. According to Yair Evron, When Israel launched its campaign against Hezbollah in 2006, it announced far reaching objectives, including a complete change of the situation in southern Lebanon and the destruction of Hezbollah. These were entirely unrealistic and certainly unattainable through military methods." Yair Evron, "Deterrence: The Campaign against Hamas," *Institute for National Strategic Studies Strategic Assessment*, Volume 11, No. 4, (2009) http://www.inss.org.il/publications. php?cat=21&incat=&read=2656; Steven Erlanger, "For Israel, 2006 Lessons But Old Pitfalls," *New York Times*, 7 January 2009. Also see, Matt M. Matthews, *We Were Caught Unprepared: The 2006 Hezbollah-Israeli War, The Long War Series Occasional Paper 26*, (Fort Leavenworth, KS: Combat Studies Institute Press, 2008).

3. Steven Erlanger, "Old Pitfalls;" Matt M. Mathews, 37; Ron Tira, e-mail interview by author, 22 January 2009.

4. Matthews, 22; Maryam al-Bassam, "Interview with Lebanese Hezbollah Leader Hasan Nasrallah," *Beirut News TV Channel* in Arabic, date of interview unknown, aired 27 August 2006, quoted in Captain Daniel Helmer's, "Not Quite Counterinsurgency: A Cautionary Tale for US Forces Based on Israel's Operation Change of Direction," *Armor*, January-February 2007, 8.

5. Amir Kulick, "Hezbollah vs. the IDF: The Operational Dimension," *Strategic Assessment*, Jaffee Center for Strategic Studies, Tel Aviv University, Vol. 9, No. 3, November 2006, 2, http://www.tau.ac.il/jcss/sa/v9n3p7Kulick.html (accessed 15 July 2007); Sergio Catignani, "The Israeli-Hezbollah Rocket War: A Preliminary Assessment," *Global Strategy Forum*, September 2006, 1, http://www.globalstrategyforum. org (accessed 1 August 2007).

6. Kulick, 3.

7. "The Hezbollah Challenge . . . An Alternate Paradigm?" Assistant Deputy Chief of Staff for Intelligence (DCSINT), US Army Training and Doctrine Command, Fort Monroe, VA, No Date; Ron Tira, e-mail interview by author, 23 September 2007.

8. Kulick, 3; Andrew Exum, "Hezbollah at War: A Military Assessment," The Washington Institute for Near East Policy, *Policy Focus* #63, December 2006, 6; "The Hezbollah Challenge . . . An Alternate Paradigm? DCSINT; "Hezbollah As A Strategic Arm of Iran." *Intelligence and Terrorism Information Center at the Center for Special Studies (C.S.S.)* 8 September 2006, 10, *http://www.terrorism-info.org.il/site/html/ search.asp?sid=13&pid=161&numResults=4&isSearch=yes&isT8=yes* (accessed 21 August 2007); "Hezbollah a North Korea-Type Guerilla Force," *Intelligence Online*, 25 August–7 September 2006, www.IntelligenceOnline.com (accessed 21 August 2007).

9. Kulick, 3.

10. Ron Tira, E-mail interview by author, 23 September 2007.

11. "The Hezbollah Challenge . . . An Alternate Paradigm? DCSINT; Kulick, 4.

12. Kulick, 4.

13. David Makovsky and Jeffrey White, "Lessons and Implications of the Israel-Hizballah War: A Preliminary Assessment," *The Washington Institute for Near East Policy*, Policy Focus No. 60, October 2006, 49.

14. "Hezbollah as a strategic arm of Iran;" "Hezbollah a North Korea-Type Guerilla Force."

15. "North Koreans Assisted Hezbollah with Tunnel Construction," *Terrorism Focus*, The Jamestown Foundation, Vol. III, Issue 30, 1 August 2006, 1.

16. Alastair Crooke and Mark Perry, "How Hezbollah Defeated Israel—Part 1: Winning the Intelligence War," *Asia Times Online*, 12 October 2006, http://atimes.com/atimes/Middle_East/HJ12Ak01.html (accessed 24 September 2007).

17. Kulick, 4-5.

18. Ron Tira, "Breaking the Amoeba's Bones," *Strategic Assessment*, Jaffee Center for Strategic Studies, Tel Aviv University, Vol. 9, No. 3, November 2006, 9.

19. Ron Tira e-mail interview, 22 September 2007.

20. Yair Evron, "Deterrence;" Charles Levinson reported that, "Two years ago in Lebanon, Israeli officials vowed to wipe out Hezbollah and bring back two kidnapped Israeli soldiers. They didn't accomplish either goal." Charles Levinson, "Israel's Ground Assault Marks Shift in Strategy," *Wall Street Journal*, 5 January 2009.

21. Winograd Committee Interim Report, (Hebrew) 66-68; The partial findings of the Winograd report stated that Halutz "failed in his duties as commander in chief of the army and as a critical part of the political-military leadership, and exhibited flaws in professionalism, responsibility and judgment." "The Winograd Report," *Haaretz.com*, 1 January 2007, http://www.haaretz.com/hasen/spages/854051.html (accessed 17 September 2007); Also see Matthews, 36-37.

22. The Chief of the General Staff, Lieutenant General Dan Halutz, was born in 1948 in Tel Aviv. He grew up in Moshav Hagor and completed his high-school studies at the "Kogel" high-school in Holon. Dan Halutz was drafted into the IDF in 1966, and volunteered for the IAF's pilot's course, which he completed in 1968 as a combat pilot. After completing a field training course on an "Oragon" plane and serving as a pilot on the "Mister 4" and "Vutour" planes he transferred, at the end of 1969, to the IAF's first "Phantom" Squadron ("The One"). He then participated in the War of Attrition, during which he completed approximately 40 operational sorties, and after which he was posted as an instructor at the IAF flight school. In 1973 Dan Halutz was released from service in the IDF. He continued to serve as a reserve pilot, which included service in the Yom Kippur War, during which he completed 43 operational sorties. After the war he returned to serve as executive officer of the "Phantom" Squadron. In 1978 Halutz was released from active duty once more, and served as a reserve pilot for four years,

during which he participated in Operation PEACE FOR GALILEE. In 1982 he returned to service and began piloting F-16 aircraft. In 1984 he received command over the "Phantom" Squadron, and two years later was appointed Head of the Operational Unit of the "Lavi" project. Dan Halutz's command positions in the IAF included Head of the Weapon Systems Department, Commander of the IAF Base "Hatzor," Head of the Air Division and Chief of the IAF Staff. He took part in the IAF's operational activities since the War of Attrition, and acquired rich operational experience, with hundreds of operational sorties which resulted in the downing of three enemy aircraft. In July of 1998 Dan Halutz was promoted to the rank of Major General and appointed Assistant Head of the General Staff Branch, in the IDF's General Staff. In April 2000 he was appointed Commander of the IAF. In July 2004 he was appointed Deputy Chief of the General Staff.In June 2005 Lieutenant General Halutz was appointed Chief of the IDF General Staff. During his service in the IAF, Halutz has accumulated approximately 4,000 flight hours. Ron Tira, private collection.

23. Matthews, 15.

24. Ibid. 24.

25. Russell W. Glenn, "All Glory Is Fleeting: Insights from the Second Lebanon War," *National Defense Research Institute*, RAND, February 2008, 18. Ron Tira, e-mail interview by author, 19 February 2009.

26. Shimon Naveh, interview by author, 1 November 2007; Colonel Ronen Shviki, interview by author, 23 February 2009.

27. Yotam Feldman, "Dr. Naveh, or How I Learned to Stop Worrying and Walk Through Walls," *Haaretz.com*, 27 October 2007, http://www.haaretz.com/hasen/spage/917158.html (accessed 5 November 2007).

28. Milan N. Vego, "Systems versus Classical Approach to Warfare," *Joint Forces Quarterly*, Issue 52, 1st Quarter 2009, 42.

29. Feldman.

30. Glenn, 19, 35.

31. Ron Tira, e-mail interview by author, 19 June 2007.

32. Naveh, interview.

33. Alex Fishman, "Struck by a Virus," *Yedioth Ahronoth*, B4, (No Date).

34. Notes from briefing by Eliot Cohen to USA CGSOC at Fort Leavenworth, KS, 17 September, 2006.

35. Yehuda Avner, "A Battalion Commander's Anger," *Jerusalem Post Online*, 22 August 2006, http://www.jpost.com/servlet/Satellite?pagename=JPost%2FJPArticle%2FShowFull&cid=1154525926212 (accessed 10 September 2007).

36. Glenn, 35.

37. Haninah Levine, "The Revolution in Military Affairs' Shocks but Does Not Awe Israeli Commission," *Center For Defense Information*, Straus Military Reform Project, 11 June 2007, 8, http://www.cdi.org/friendlyversion/printversion.cfm?documentID=3977 (accessed 20 September 2007).

38. Ron Tira, e-mail interview by author, 21 June 2007.

39. Uri Bar-Joseph, "Their Most Humiliating Hour," *Haaretz.com*, 27 April 2007, http://www.haaretz.com/hasen/spages/853115.html (accessed 19 September 2007).

40. Naveh, interview.

41. Ron Tira, e-mail interview by author, 16 August 2007.

42. Levine.

43. Uzi Mahnaimi, "Humbling of the Supertroops Shatters Israeli Army Morale," *TimesOnLine*, 27 August 2006, http://www.timesonline.co.uk/tol/news/world/article620874.ece (accessed 19 September 2007).

44. Crooke and Perry, "Part 1: Winning the Intelligence War," 5.

45. Scott Wilson, "Israeli War Plan Had No Exit Strategy," *WashingtonPost.com*, http://www.washingtonpost.com/wp-dyn/content/article/2006/10/20/AR2006102001688_pf.html (accessed 24 September 2007).

46. Alastair Crooke and Mark Perry, "How Hezbollah Defeated Israel—Part 2: Winning the Ground War," *Asia Times Online*, 12 October 2006, http://atimes.com/atimes/Middle_East/HJ12Ak01.html (accessed 24 September 2007).

47. Exum, 9.

48. Alex Fishman, "The Changing Face of the IDF: The Security Agenda and the Ballot Box," *Strategic Assessment*, Jaffee Center for Strategic Studies, Vol. 8, No. 4, February 2006, 6, http://www.tau.ac.il/jcss/sa/v8n4p3Fishman.html (accessed 25 September 2007).

49. Mahnaimi.

50. Ibid.

51. Exum, 10.

52. *Jerusalem Post*, 24 July 2006.

53. Exum, 10.

54. Crooke and Perry, "Part 2: Winning the Ground War," 2.

55. Ibid.

56. Helmer.

57. Greg Myre, "Risks Escalate As Israel Fights A Ground War," *New York Times*, 5 August 2006, http://www.nytimes.com/2006/08/05/world/middleeast/05zone.html (accessed 1 October 2007); Crooke and Perry, "Part 2: Winning the Ground War," 5.

58. Jonathan Finer, "Israeli Soldiers Find a Tenacious Foe in Hezbollah," *WashingtonPost.com*, 8 August 2006, http://www.washingtonpost.com/wp-dyn/content/article/2006/08/07/AR2006080701453.html (accessed 9 October 2007), 1-4.

59. Crooke and Perry, "Part 2: Winning the Ground War," 10.

60. Mahnaimi, 5.

61. "Security Council Calls For End To Hostilities Between Hezbollah, Israel," *United Nations Security Council SC/8808*, 11 August 2006, http://www.un.org/News/Press/docs/2006/sc8808.doc.htm (accessed 10 October 2007).

62. Ron Tira, e-mail interview by author, 11 July 2007.

63. Ibid.

64. Nava Tzuriel and Eitan Glickman, translated by Adam Keller, "The Canyon of Death," *Yediot Aharonot*, 16 August 2006, 1, http://www.kibush.co.il/show_file. asp?num=15859 (accessed 1 October 2007).

65. Josh Brannon, "Halutz slammed for promoting Lebanon war generals," *Jerusalem Post Online*, 30 October 2007, http://www.jpost.com/servlet/Satellite?page name=JPost%2FJPArticle%2FShowFull&cid=1161811237367 (accessed 5 October 2007); Amos Harel, "Seven Months On, The IDF Implementing Lessons of the Lebanon War," *haaretz.com*, http://www.haaretz.com/hasen/spages/822989.html (accessed 7 October 2007); Yossi Yehoshua, "Lebanon War Commander Resigns," *YnetNews. com*, 1 June 2007, http://www.ynetnews.com/articles/0,7340,L-3407286,00.html (accessed 7 October 2007).

66. Yaakov Katz, "Commanders Failed to Fulfill Missions," *Jerusalem Post Online*, 15 October 2006, http://www.jpost.com/servlet/Satellite?cid=1159193446682&p agename=JPost%2FJPArticle%2FShowFull (accessed 11 October 2007).

67. Ron Tira, e-mail interview by author, 19 June 2007.

68. Helmer, 7-11.

69. Yaakov Katz, "Post-battle Probe Finds Merkava Tank Misused in Lebanon," *Jerusalem Post Online*, 3 September 2006, http://www.jpost.com/servlet/Satellite?c id=1154525995589&pagename=JPost%2FJPArticle%2FPrinter (accessed 5 October 2007).

70. Tzuriel and Glickman, "The Canyon of Death." This ambush was video-taped by the Hezbollah camera crews that accompany every combat unit. The action and interviews with the Hezbollah missilemen can be viewed on various websites.

71. Helmer, 10.

72. Tzuriel and Glickman, "The Canyon of Death," 2.

73. Yaakov Katz, "Wadi Saluki Battle—Microcosm of War's Mistakes," *Jerusalem Post Online*, 29 August 2006, http://www.jpost.com/servlet/Satellite?cid=115 4525969154&pagename=JPost%2FJPArticle%2FShowFull (accessed 15 September 2007), 1-2.

74. Ibid., 2.

75. Helmer, 9-10; Tzuriel and Glickman, "The Canyon of Death," 2.

76. Katz, "Wadi Saluki Battle," 2.

77. Harel, "Seven Months On."

78. Yehoshua, "Lebanon War Commander Resigns."

79. Katz, "Commanders Failed to Fulfill Missions."

80. Crooke and Perry, "Part 2: Winning the Ground War," 9.

81. Mahnaimi, 5; Exum, 12.

82. Matthews, 85; Winograd Committee Final Report, Israel Ministry of Foreign Affairs, 30 January 2008.

83. Biography: Amir Peretz, Israel Ministry of Foreign Affairs, http://www.mfa. gov.il/MFA/Government/Personalities/From+A-Z/Amir+Peretz.htm (accessed 19 February 2009); "IDF Chief Halutz Resigns," *YNetNews.com*, http://www.ynet.co.il/ english/articles/0,7340,L-3353269,00.html (accessed 19 February 2009).

84. Glenn, 40.

85. Matthews, 36; Biography: Ehud Barak, Israel Ministry of Foreign Affairs, http://www.mfa.gov.il/MFA/MFAArchive/2000_2009/2001/3/Ehud+Barak.htm (accessed 19 February 2009).

86. Lieutenant General Gabi Ashkenazi was born in 1954 in Moshav Hagor (Israel).

- 1972–Ashkenazi was recruited into the Golani Brigade
- 1973–During the Yom Kippur War Ashkenazi participated in the battles along the southern front
- 1976–He participated in the Entebbe Operation
- 1978–Served as a deputy battalion commander in the Golani Brigade and was wounded while participating in the Litani Operation
- 1979-1980–Took part in the Barak Command and Staff Course, which he completed with honors
- 1980–Ashkenazi was appointed Commander of a Golani Battalion and in 1981 received the rank of Lieutenant Colonel
- 1982–During the Lebanon War, Ashkenazi was appointed Deputy Commander of the Golani Brigade. He commanded the forces that captured Beaufort, Nabatiyah and Jebel Baruch.
- 1983-1984–He participated in the Command and Staff Course of the US Marines
- 1984–Ashkenazi was appointed Operations Officer at the Headquarters of the Infantry and Paratrooper Corps
- 1985–He was raised to the rank of Colonel and became the Commander of a Regional Brigade in the Northern Command
- 1987–Ashkenazi was appointed Commander of the Golani Brigade
- 1988–Ashkenazi was appointed Operations Officer of the Northern Command
- 1990–He was transferred to the Armored Corps, raised to the rank of Brigadier General and was appointed Commander of a Reserve Armored Division in the Northern Command
- 1992–He was appointed Commander of the IDF Liaison Unit to Lebanon
- 1994–He was appointed Commander of the IDF Operations Unit within the General Staff
- 1996–Ashkenazi was promoted to Major General and served as Assistant Head of the General Staff Branch, in the General Staff
- 1998–Ashkenazi was appointed GOC Northern Command
- 2002–He was appointed Deputy Chief of Staff

• 2005–Ashkenazi retired from the IDF

On February 4th 2007, the Government of Israel decided to appoint Gabi Ashkenazi to be the 19th Chief of the General Staff. On February 14th 2007, Gabi Ashkenazi received the rank of Lieutenant General and was appointed Chief of Staff. Lieutenant General Ashkenazi holds a Bachelors Degree in Political Science from the University of Haifa and is a graduate of the Harvard Business Management program for senior executives. He is married to Ronit and is the father of Gali and Itai. (Author's Collection).

87. "Who is Gabi Ashkenazi?" *YNetNews.com*, 22 January 2007, http://www.ynet.co.il/english/articles/0,7340,L-3355253,00.html (accessed 19 February 2009); "Ashkenazi, Gabi—IDF Chief of Staff," *YNetnews.com*, 8 February 2007, http://www.ynet.co.il/english/articles/0,7340,L-3362535,00.html (accessed 20 February 2009).

88. "Armed Forces, Israel," *Jane's Sentinel Security Assessment—Eastern Mediterranean*, 13 January 2009.

89. Hanan Greenberg, "IDF Chief Appoints Special Team to Study Winograd Report," *YNetNews.com*, http://www.ynet.co.il/english/articles/0,7340,L-3500824,00.html (accessed 23 February 2009).

90. Ron Tira, e-mail interview by author, 26 January 2009.

91. Alon Ben-David, "Debriefing Teams Brand IDF Doctrine 'Completely Wrong,'" *Jane's Defence Weekly*, 3 January 2007.

92. Ron Tira, e-mail interview by author, 26 January 2009.

93. Yehuda Wegman, "The Distorted Self-Image: On the IDF and Its Responsibility for Civilians," *Strategic Assessment*, August 2007, Vol. 10, No.2, 2.

94. Ron Tira, e-mail interview by author, 26 January 2009.

95. Yaakov Katz, "IDF applying lessons of war to improve use of tanks," *Jerusalem Post*, 20 March 2007.

96. Ibid.

97. Major General Custer, "Briefing on Israeli Operations in Gaza," (lecture, Lewis and Clark Center, 5 February 2009).

98. *Jane's Sentinel Security Assessment—Eastern Mediterranean*, 17 December 2008; Yoaz Hendel, "The Reserves Comeback," *Strategic Assessment*, February 2008, Vol. 10, No.4, 2.

99. Ibid.

100. Yaakov Katz, "Army to Upgrade Reservist Equipment," *Jerusalem Post*, 20 March 2007.

101. *Jane's Information Group*; *Jane's World Insurgency And Terrorism, Hamas*.

102. Anthony H. Cordesman, "The 'Gaza War:' A Strategic Analysis," *Center For Strategic & International Studies*, Final Review Draft: Circulated for Comment and Updating, 2 February 2009, 5.

103. Ibid, 8.

104. Ron Tira, e-mail interview by author, 28 February 2009.

105. Colonel Hanny Caspi, "Cast Lead Operation," Briefing slides; Colonel (RET) John Antal, "Flashpoint Gaza: The Israeli Defense Forces (IDF) Launches 'Operation Cast Lead,'" *ArmchairGeneral.com*, http://www.armchairgeneral.com/flashpoint-gaza-analysis-january-4-2009.htm, 5-6, (accessed 1 March 2009).

106. Ibid.

107. Ron Tira, e-mail interview by author, 28 February 2009.

108. Ron Tira, e-mail interview by author, 9 March 2009.

109. Ron Tira, e-mail interview by author, 22 January 2009.

110. Cordesman, 8-9.

111. Cordesman, 15.

112. Custer Briefing; Ehud Eiran, e-mail interview by author, 23 January 2009.

113. Mohammed Najib, "Hamas Investigates Poor Military Response to IDF," *Jane's Defence Weekly*, 28 January 2009, 16.

114. Cordesman, 9.

115. Cordesman, 15; "Operation Cast Lead—Update No. 1," Intelligence and Terrorism Information Center at the Israel Intelligence Heritage & Commemoration Center, 28 December 2008, 4; "IDF Operations in the Gaza Strip," *Daily Update*, 27 December 2008, The Military-Strategic Information Section/The Strategic Division.

116. Ibid.; Cordesman, 16.

117. "Operation Cast Lead—Update No. 2, Intelligence and Terrorism Information Center at the Israel Intelligence Heritage & Commemoration Center, 29 December 2008, 4; Cordesman, 21; Ron Tira, email interview by author, 22 January 2009.

118. Cordesman, 19.

119. Cordesman, 27, 28, 38.

120. Israel Ministry of Defense, http://www.globalsecurity.org/military/library/news/2009/01/mil-090103-idf01.htm (accessed 2 March 2009).

121. Cordesman, 38.

122. Two territorial brigades.

123. Colonel Ronen Shviki, e-mail interview by author 9 March 2009.

124. Ibid; Cordesman, 39.

125. Ron Tira, e-mail interview by author, 26 January 2009; Aaron J. Klein, "Israel Enters Gaza: Negotiating with Extreme Prejudice," *Time*, 4 January 2009.

126. Ibid, 41.

127. Ron Tira, e-mail interview by author, 22 January 2009.

128. Klein, "Israel Enters Gaza;" Joel J. Sprayregen, "The Inside Story of Operation Cast Lead," *American Thinker*, 27 January 2009, http://www.americanthinker.com/2009/01/inside_story_of_israels_succes.html; Cordesman, 39-40.

129. Klein, "Israel Enters Gaza;" Sprayregen, "The Inside Story;" Cordesman, 39-40.

130. Levinson, "Israel's Ground Assault Marks Shift in Strategy."

131. Mohammed Najib, "Hamas Investigates Poor Military Response to IDF," *Jane's Defence Weekly*, 28 January 2009, 16.

132. Sprayregen, "The Inside Story."

133. Cordesman, 41.

134. Ron Tira, e-mail interview by author, 22 January 2009.

135. Cordesman, 42; "IDF Operations in Gaza: Cast Lead," Israel Ministry of Foreign Affairs, 21 January 2009, under "5 January Friendly Fire Incident," http://www.mfa.gov.il/MFA/Terrorism-+Obstacle+to+Peace/Terrorism+and+Islamic+Fundamentalism-/Aerial_strike_weapon_development_center+_Gaza_28-Dec-2008.htm (accessed 9 March 2009).

136. "IDF Operations in Gaza: Cast Lead," Israel Ministry of Foreign Affairs, under "Summary of Today's IDF Operations," http://www.mfa.gov.il/MFA/Terrorism-+Obstacle+to+Peace/Terrorism+and+Islamic+Fundamentalism-/Aerial_strike_weapon_development_center+_Gaza_28-Dec-2008.htm (accessed 10 March 2009).

137. Najib, "Hamas Investigates Poor Military Response to IDF," 16.

138. Ron Tira, e-mail interview by author, 22 January 2009.

139. Ibid.

140. Hanan Greenberg, "Top Officer: Activity Efficient For Limited Amount of Time," *YNetNews.com*, 13 January 2009, http://www.ynet.co.il/english/articles/0,7340,L-3655094,00.html (accessed 10 March 2009).

141. Arnon Ben-Dror, "Reserve Forces Joining the Operation," *Israel Defense Forces*, http://dover.idf.il/IDF/English/News/the_Front/09/01/1302.htm (accessed 8 March 2009).

142. "Operation Cast Lead IDF Operations in the Gaza Strip: Daily Update–Day 9, 4 January 2009," Military-Strategic Information Section/The Strategic Division, Distributed 0500 14 January 2009, ftp://www.jcrcny.org/jcrc/pdf/gaza/LFRD-IDF_Update_040109_ppt.pdf.

143. Ibid.; Greenberg, "Top Officer: Activity Efficient For Limited Amount of Time," Cordesman, 57.

144. "IDF Principles of War," *Jewish Virtual Library*, http://www.jewishvirtuallibrary.org/jsource/Society_&_Culture/IDFprinciplesofwar.html (accessed 13 March 2009).

Chapter 2

Hamas and Hezbollah:

A Comparison of Tactics

by
Ms. Penny L. Mellies
TRADOC Intelligence Support Activity

Introduction

The US Army wisely spends a great deal of time analyzing lessons learned and comparing the tactics, techniques, and procedures (TTPs) of past conflicts. The dust barely settles before analysts begin looking for relevant lessons learned and unique nuances of the most recent conflict hoping to glean insight. While there is undoubtedly great value in this approach, it will never fully capture the dynamic elements of each event until the incident is put into proper context. Such analysis is incomplete without a consideration of each belligerent's environment which allows us to understand the conditions that contribute to the conflict or war under review. Without understanding the unique environment in which each belligerent operates, it is impossible to derive accurate and valuable insight.

The purpose of this chapter is to explore the operational environments (OEs) of Hamas and Hezbollah, and present a comparison of the tactics, techniques, and procedures (TTPs) used in The Second Lebanon War in 2006 between Hezbollah and Israel and the Hamas/Israeli conflict with emphasis on the 2008-2009 Operation CAST LEAD, respectively. The chapter explores key TTP similarities and differences between these organizations and does not discuss Israel's actions or responses in either conflict. The goal is to focus exclusively on Hamas and Hezbollah and their unique OEs and TTPs.

Application of the PMESII + PT Variables

As a framework, this comparison utilizes the TRADOC G2 TRISA-Threats operational environment analysis (OEA) methodology—taking the eight variables of the contemporary operational environment (COE) and applying each to Hamas and Hezbollah. These COE variables are the familiar PMESII + PT[1]: *P*olitical, *M*ilitary, *E*conomic, *S*ocial, *I*nfrastructure, *I*nformation, *P*hysical environment and *T*ime. The variables represent the conditions within a selected OE and therefore provide an understanding of the belligerent based on the unique conditions within each environment. The PMESII + PT process is merely a comprehensive view of the human terrain in the manner one evaluates and visualizes the effects of physical terrain and weather using the OAKOC (*O*bservation and fields of fire, *A*venues of approach, *K*ey terrain, *O*bstacles and movement, *C*over and concealment) appreciation.[2] By defining the makeup of these variables as they relate to the specific OE, the nature and characteristics of that environment and actions are distilled.

Once each belligerent's environment is defined, a true analysis of the similarities and differences can begin to be constructed. Simply put, a fuller understanding of each belligerent gives us better insight into that belligerent's tactical actions. Each conflict can then be put into context—resulting in better analysis. Localized tactical events must be related to localized conditions and localized conditions are defined by the variables of the OE.

Hamas and Hezbollah

The US Department of State designates both the radical Palestinian Sunni Hamas organization and the Lebanese Shiite group Hezbollah as Foreign Terrorist Organizations (FTOs). While this highlights that there are inherent similarities between the groups, they operate under unique confines that can be better understood after a thorough analysis of each group's actions and tactics. Both organizations' recent military history with Israel provides an opportunity for such an analysis. The following section identifies the nature and characteristics of the OEs of Hamas and Hezbollah. It's important to note, though, that while both of these non-state belligerents have a global presence, this chapter only focuses upon those elements of Hamas operating in the OE of the Gaza Strip and Hezbollah operating in the OE of Lebanon.

Hamas is an acronym for *Harakat al-Muqawamah al-Islamiyyah* (Islamic Resistance Movement). Founded in 1987, Hamas is a militant Sunni Palestinian organization operating primarily in the Gaza Strip and parts of the West Bank. The group's followers are opposed to the existence of Israel, and believe that it is the religious duty of every Muslim to assist in the return of all Israeli-controlled territory to the Palestinians. Hamas is part militant fighting force, part Sunni political party and part social service organization that has a growing influence in its OE.

An overarching *Shura* council provides organizational guidance and oversight for the organization as a whole. Hamas is composed of three overlapping "wings" or sections—the social services/welfare section, the political bureau and the military wing. The political bureau, led by Khalad Mashal, is located in Damascus, Syria. Mashal's deputy, Mousa Abu Marzouk, operates in the Gaza Strip.

The political bureau, which is the public political face of Hamas, is composed of 8-12 members and oversees the combat elements (Qassam Brigades) and social services section. Despite public pronouncements of such organizational boundaries, the divisions are operationally less significant. Missions, personnel and resources flow between the sections with the military component ultimately garnering the most attention and funding. The fighting section, as the group's name states, defines it is the heart and soul of Hamas.

Although categorized as a non-state actor, in many respects Hamas acts like a traditional political party by providing public services and social programs to the local population and participating in the Palestinian political process. On January 25, 2006, Hamas won 74 out of 132 seats in the Palestinian parliamentary election[3] and the following year it seized power from Fatah in the Gaza Strip in a bloody *coup d'état*. Today, Hamas is the dominant political, social, economic and military force operating in Gaza.

Hezbollah, whose name means *"Party of God,"* is the older of the two organizations, being founded in 1982. The group's objectives include the establishment of a Shiite theocracy in Lebanon, the destruction of Israel, and the elimination of western influences from the Middle East. The US Director of National Intelligence (DNI), retired Admiral Dennis Blair, defines Hezbollah as "a multifaceted, disciplined organization that combines political, social, paramilitary and terrorist elements."[4] The DNI also foresees that "in any potential future conflict, Hezbollah is likely to be better prepared and more capable than in 2006" as it continues to adapt and hone its fighting skills and incorporate lessons learned from its past engagements.[5] Over the decades, Hezbollah has not only professionalized its military capabilities but joined Lebanon's political process and enmeshed itself into the fabric of Lebanese society. Like Hamas, Hezbollah is a global entity, but Hezbollah's reach and depth of operations is more developed.

Hezbollah's global presence is amplified by its substantial Iranian political and financial support. Iran supports both groups, but Hezbollah is clearly favored due to the fact that the founding of Hezbollah was one of revolutionary Iran's first acts, their shared Shia adherence, and importantly, Hezbollah's successes.[6] The current intelligence community position is that "Hizbollah [sic] is the largest recipient of Iranian financial aid, training, and weaponry, and Iran's senior leadership has cited Hizbollah [sic] as a model for other militant groups."[7] With this backing, Hezbollah has successfully established its presence across to the globe, including the United States.

Political

From the outside the groups appear similar as radical Islamic elements seeking political cover for their military aspirations. Both are trained and supplied by the key regional powers of Iran and Syria. Indeed, the groups share traits across the political, military, economic and social spectrum. Though non-state actors, both groups have become a "state-within-a-state", taking advantage of weak and corrupt local governments to advance their political, economic, and military aims. Both groups have stepped into broken societies to provide basic services such as health care, food aid, employment opportunities, and the construction of mosques and schools. Consequently they have been rewarded with elected positions in their host governments and widespread admiration in the *Ummah* (the Muslim world or "community of believers"). Despite their adherence to differing religious doctrine, the Sunni Hamas and Shia Hezbollah work together by sharing financial resources, equipment and tactics.

Hamas has become much more than a military force, weaving itself into key positions across Gazan society. It seeks to gain legitimacy as a political belligerent in both Gaza and the West Bank. Hamas joined the political process when it entered the Palestinian parliamentary election in 2006. The organization was not seeking to create a Palestinian state in the Gaza Strip, but rather sought to form an Islamic state to replace Israel.

In 2007 a Palestinian National Unity Government was formed under Hamas leader Ismail Haniya. Later that year Hamas "succeeded in a violent takeover of all military and governmental institutions in the Gaza Strip", the aforementioned coup.[8] However, as a Center for Strategic and International Studies (CSIS) report notes, "this victory occurred far more because of a lack of leadership and elementary competence on the part of the Fatah/Palestinian Authority Forces than any great skill on the part of Hamas."[9] As a current IDF Colonel explains: "There really isn't any alternative to Hamas. Fatah is a proven failure and at least Hamas is attempting reconstruction with Iranian money versus stealing it like Fatah did."[10] Hamas shrewdly capitalized on Fatah's weaknesses, the Israeli political paralysis and Western blindness, and successfully convinced the Gazan population it could provide needed political and economic improvements. Hamas saw a political opportunity and seized it.

Hamas, whose political control extends only over the Gaza Strip, uses both social and religious programs to solidify its political legitimacy. However, support for Hamas in the Gaza Strip isn't as strong as it sometimes appears: a January 2009 report reveals: "on the streets of Gaza, support for Hamas remains strong, but in private, expressions of anger, fear and exhaustion are heard."[11] The cause of this frustration may stem from the death and destruction in Gaza caused by the recent conflict with Israel combined with Hamas' inability to improve the living conditions of Gazans. Unlike Hezbollah in southern Lebanon, Hamas appears not to have made the transition "from Islamic governance to good governance."[12]

As public support for Hamas has withered in Gaza, political unity within the group is also faltering. While Hamas leadership claims cohesion, there is evidence of increasing and significant political tension within the organization. According to the Washington Institute for Near East Policy, friction exists "between the groups' internal leadership on the ground in the Palestinian territories and its external leadership in Damascus, between leaders in the West Bank and those in Gaza, and between religious Palestinian nationalists and radical Islamists."[13] While most day-to-day decisions are made by the leadership in Damascus they now face increasing resistance from the leaders in Gaza. Deputy Mousa Abu Marzouk's "more moderate stance" is perceived as creating a rift between himself and his boss, Meshal.[14] This difference of opinion may be causing a lack of clear or timely guidance from the highest levels of leadership and may have negatively affected Hamas' ability to act during its recent combat with Israel. However, according to Matthew Levitt of the Washington Institute for Near East Policy, "the most significant fault line with Hamas is between those who prioritize the Palestinian national cause and those who prioritize the group's Islamist ideology."[15] This tension may prove to be the most troublesome for Hamas as it attempts to be both a legitimate political force and terrorist organization. Politically, Hamas has been successful at gaining power, but the question remains whether it can translate this into the political capital in Gaza and the West Bank to follow a more extremist path.

By comparison, Hezbollah appears to have a much more unified leadership—or is, at the very least, able to keep such dissension private. This Shia-dominated political party and militant organization has actively participated in Lebanon's political system since 1992. Like Hamas, it has muscled itself in key posts across Lebanese society. According to one analysis, "Hezbollah can be active on four tracks simultaneously—the political, the social, the guerilla, and the terrorist—because its Iranian leaders are masters of long-term strategic subversion."[16] Like Hamas, Hezbollah skillfully uses social and religious programs and economic aid to gain popular support and establish political legitimacy in their OEs.

Sayyed Hassan Nasrallah is Hezbollah's Secretary General and seems to enjoy uncontested power. Numbers vary, but most estimates claim that Hezbollah has up to 10,000 active members and 30,000 supporters.[17] As mentioned, Iran directly influences the political and military decision-making and strategic agenda of both Hezbollah and Hamas. However, as Hezbollah has matured and become dominant as a Lebanese political party, there is some question concerning the depth to which Iran is now able to sway Hezbollah's political decisions and military strategies. However, even if Iranian influence is dwindling in Lebanon, Iran and Syria remain key partners of both Hamas and Hezbollah and will continue to use each other for mutual benefit.

Military

Since 2007, when Hamas gained control of the Gaza Strip, Gaza police and internal security forces and the Hamas military (the Qassam Brigades) have fallen under a joint command headed by Ahmed Jaabari.[18] This allowed a unification of forces and established more effective command of Hamas' military capability. Once unified, Hamas began to focus on a military buildup in Gaza. The focus shifted toward acquisition of advanced weapon systems such as longer-range rockets (from Iran), advanced anti-tank guided missiles (ATGMs) and increasingly powerful improvised explosive devices (IEDs). Yet, despite this unification of effort and focus on advanced systems, in 2008 the Israeli Defense Force (IDF) stated that it would "take a number of years" before the full effects of this build up would be felt.[19] The coming conflict with Israel would prove this to be true.

The Qassam Brigades are the primary military organization operating in Gaza, but are not alone. In addition to Hamas, the Palestinian Islamic Jihad (PIJ) (more than 1,000 fighters) and the Popular Resistance Committee (PRC) (a few hundred fighters) are active in Gaza and at times work directly with Hamas.[20] Both groups have targeted Israel with rocket and mortar fire.

Though estimates vary, the strength of the Qassam Brigades is believed to be between 6,000-10,000 fighters and thousands of part-time fighters— bringing the total potential fighting force to as many as 20,000.[21] However, only a few hundred can be categorized as highly proficient Hamas fighters and leaders.[22] Most of this latter group has participated in training in Syria and Iran and/or with Hezbollah in Lebanon.

Hamas divides Gaza into four operational sectors: northern (primary launch site for rockets), central, Gaza City and southern. Typical Hamas tactical actions have included suicide bombings, indirect rocket and mortar fire, small arms fire, ambushes, raids to destroy positions or abduct personnel, use of IEDs, surface-to-air fire (SAFIRE). They also have a highly competent internet presence and information operations (IO) capability.

Hamas is reported to have the following weapons: various Russian, US and Israeli small-arms and sniper rifles, grenades, ATGMs, rocket-propelled grenades (RPGs), IEDs, large amounts of explosives, various mortar and rockets (ranging from homemade Qassams to the more advanced long-range 122-mm Katyusha rockets acquired from Iran). Hamas has reportedly obtained "air defense missiles and weapons—including the SA-7 and HN-5, and RPG-29s and possibly anti-tank guided missiles . . . from Iran, Syria, and the Hezbollah."[23] In addition, Hamas used an extensive network of tunnels, IEDs, and a "spider web of prepared strong points, underground hidden shelters, and ambush points throughout urban and built up areas as defensive strong points" in the preparation of a fight with Israel.[24] Weapons, money and fighters originating in Iran and Syria are also smuggled into the Gaza Strip through this network. Israeli intelligence estimates that "some 250 tons of explosives, 80 tons of fertilizer, 4,000 rocket-propelled grenades, and 1,800 rockets were transported from Egypt to Gaza from September 2005 to December 2008."[25] This arms smuggling network is directed by Hamas and aided by the Iranian Islamic Revolutionary Guard Corps (IRGC).

Yet, given all of this, Hamas does not appear to have a group of battle-tested fighters. Unlike Hezbollah commandos, who impressed both Israelis and US military analysts, Hamas fighters appeared to be poorly trained and uncommitted to fighting IDF elements. In the recent conflict between Israel and Hamas, the IDF was able to cordon off Gaza City and other larger villages to the south within the first hours of the Israeli's thrust into Gaza. One IDF soldier observed: "we kept hearing Hamas was a strong terror organization, but it was much easier than we thought it would be . . . Hamas fighters are just villagers with guns. They don't even aim when they shoot."[26] Reports indicate that the commander of Hamas' rocket forces in Gaza City was forced to fire mortars himself after junior Hamas operatives refused to go outside fearing an Israeli strike.[27]

According to the Center for Strategic and International Studies, "unlike Hezbollah, Hamas never had to develop the combat skills necessary to fight an effective opponent."[28] Much of Hezbollah's combat skills can be attributed to the existence of established Hezbollah training sites in Lebanon—staffed by foreigners, most notably IRGC advisors and trainers. Geographically, the crowded Gaza Strip does not afford such training opportunities.

Like Hezbollah, Hamas has effectively used rockets and mortars to attack and harass Israeli cities. During both the conflicts, Israel was unable to stop the rocket attacks. Yet, in terms of military power, Hamas simply lacks the combat power and effectiveness of Hezbollah. Hamas' military training is not as advanced as that provided to Hezbollah forces, nor does Hamas receive the most advanced weapons from its sponsors. Hamas generally lacks the sophistication of Hezbollah, and has proven more susceptible to Israeli targeting. A recent RAND study concludes that overall "Hezbollah retains a stronger, more capable, fighting force. While Hamas primarily operates as a traditional insurgency group, Hezbollah can manifest both insurgent-like skills and more-conventional operational and tactical skills."[29]

Hezbollah's military wing, the Islamic Resistance (IR), can be divided into two types of fighters: the so-called "elite," or core fighters—numbering between 300 and 1,000 (perhaps as many as 3,000)[30]; and local fighters that can be called to action as needed. The number of local fighters cannot be accurately estimated, because they often include many not formally associated with Hezbollah, but the number may be as high as 10,000.[31] Both Hamas and Hezbollah claim the ability to easily increase its fighting force size—by relying on the willingness of the local population to join the fight. Hezbollah organizes its fighters into small, self-sufficient teams capable of operating independently and without direction from higher authority for long periods of time. The most significant aspect of Hezbollah's organization is the high degree of autonomy given to junior leaders. This is a function of Iranian doctrinal influences and the entrepreneurial nature of Lebanese society.

Hezbollah's weapons inventory includes massive amounts of artillery rockets (Zelzal-2, the Nazeat, the Fajr-3 and -5, 302-mm, 220-mm, 122-mm, 107-mm); ATGMs (ranging from the AT-14, AT-5, AT-13 METIS-M, AT-3, AT-4, Milan, TOW, RPG-29 and the RPG-7); surface-to-air missiles; and anti-ship missiles.[32] Hezbollah also posses an unmanned aerial vehicle (UAV) fleet, including 30 Mirsad-1 UAVs from Iran, that gives it an impressive long-range sensor-to-shooter link.[33] Exact numbers are hard to ascertain, but sources believe that Hezbollah has replenished much of pre-2006 munitions inventory since the end of the latest conflict with Israel.[34] The best-known weapon in Hezbollah's inventory is the Katushya rocket, some models of which have a range of 45 miles that has been used repeatedly against Israel. Prewar estimates indicated that Hezbollah had accumulated up to 12,000 munitions, the vast majority of which were the Katushya.[35] The rockets are notoriously inaccurate, but they served as an area-effect weapon intended to terrorize Israeli citizens and taunt the Israeli military, demonstrating the myth of Israel's military invincibility—Israel's prime strategic asset.[36] Hezbollah enjoys a wider range of weapons then Hamas, notably in terms of more anti-tank weapons, and UAVs.[37]

Both Hamas and Hezbollah are the foremost practitioners and adherents to the military doctrine of *Muqawama*, or resistance. This doctrine is based on an "ideological view according to which Israel is particularly unable and unwilling to absorb causalities and make sacrifices."[38] Put simply a war of attrition favors the insurgent Islamists. Unlike Hamas, Hezbollah's recent actions against Israel showed it to be an effective fighting force on many levels. Hezbollah remains the only Arab or Muslim entity to successfully face the Israelis in combat and this provides them with tremendous military cachet.

Economic

Hamas and Hezbollah have thrived in no small measure because of the poor economic conditions within their OEs. The poor economies in Gaza and Lebanon have aided the groups' ability to attract members and gain prominence in their respective political circles. The limited economic opportunities of these OEs, however, require Hezbollah and Hamas to turn to Iran, Syria and black market sources for economic support.

Hamas operates in the grinding poverty of the Gaza Strip. The CIA estimates that the unemployment rate is over 41%; the inflation rate is at 11.5 %, and 80% of the population lives below the poverty line.[39] The already fragile economy was further weakened in 2007, when land and sea borders to Gaza were sealed by Israel and Egypt, in response to Hamas' coup. This blockade has led to complete economic devastation, massive business and industry closure and shortages of food and other basic items. Currently, 75% of the population is dependent upon the United Nations' World Food Program (WFP) for survival.[40]

This dire economic situation has been used by Hamas to reinforce its IO message, to garner additional international support and aid, and as a tool for local recruitment. However, an ironic juxtaposition remains: while Hamas actively advocates the destruction of Israel, Hamas is, as shown by the results of the blockade, entirely dependent upon the Israeli economy for energy, raw materials and employment. Many of its financial institutions are tied to Israeli banks. Gaza requires the Israeli Electronic Corporation for the majority of its electrical power, which led to an increased vulnerability in Gaza during the recent conflict. This electricity from Israel powers everything from sewage treatment plants to the smuggling tunnels' lighting and ventilation. Though Hamas' capabilities suffer when electricity is shut off, the situation simultaneously gives Hamas leverage over the Gazan population because it operates the tunnels that supply food and generator fuel.

Hamas survives in the harsh economy through the use of alternative sources of income and external funding sources. Smuggling tunnels, regional and global charities, and its own system of taxes and customs fees on smuggled goods are all used to generate income, assist with social charities and, most importantly, to develop its military might.[41] Much like Hezbollah, Hamas operates "a network of fund-raising organizations in Europe and the United States," along with funds received from Saudi Arabia, Iran and Syria.[42]

Efforts to raise money through its criminal ties are also beneficial to Hamas. A recent publication focusing on the connection between terror and criminal organizations concluded that "nineteen of the forty-three designated FTOs are linked definitively to the global drug trade, and up to 60% of terror organizations are suspected of being connected in some fashion with the illegal narcotics trade."[43] Hamas and Hezbollah operations in the Tri-Border region (where the borders of Argentina, Brazil and Paraguay intersect) of South America are an excellent example of this connectivity and coordinated effort between criminal and terrorist organizations.

Hezbollah, by contrast, enjoys a more stable economic base of operations. The economy is hardly robust, but is functioning much better the Gazan economy. Still, unemployment is at roughly 9% of the population and 28% of people live at or below the poverty level and provides an excellent breeding ground for recruits.[44] The rate of inflation is at 10%. However, the 2006 conflict caused significant damage to the infrastructure and totaling an estimated 3.6 billion worth of damage across Lebanon.[45]

Like Hamas, Hezbollah operates a variety of overt, covert and fraudulent charities to raise funds and exploits connections with criminal organizations to conduct narco-trafficking, and smuggles gold and diamonds. According to the IDF, Hezbollah also smuggles arms with Fatah, Hamas and the Palestinian Authority (PA).[46] As mentioned, the group also receives external funding from Iran, Syria, the Lebanese expatriate community and other radical elements worldwide. Much of this is facilitated by the far-flung Lebanese expatriate community and global information and communications technologies (ICTs) which foster the rapid flow of ideologies and cash.

Social

Much like the economic conditions in these OEs, the social climate in the Gaza Strip and Lebanon allow insurgent groups to thrive. Like Hezbollah, Hamas attempts to provide "state-like" services to the population in hopes of securing support. Much of the appeal of Hamas stems from this social involvement, particularly during the organization's early history. Compared to Hezbollah's social activity, however, Hamas' level of support provided is small.[47]

Hamas' Gaza social programs serve a population that is young and largely made up of refugees. According to CIA data, the population of the Gaza Strip is 1.5 million, with more than 1 million classified as Palestinian refugees[48]—*and 45% of the Gaza population is 14 years of age and younger.*[49] The predominant ethnic group—at 99%—is Palestinian Arab. The declining economy's ever-dwindling job opportunities coupled with demographics create a fertile ground for Hamas recruitment of young men willing to risk death in exchange for financial support for their families. It also allows Hamas to use civilian assistance as a defensive shield during attacks. For example, several reports state that Hamas used civilians positioned on rooftops to shield critical buildings from Israeli air strikes.[50]

Lebanon's population is over four million.[51] Close to 26% of the population of Lebanon is 14 years of age and younger.[52] Like Hamas, Hezbollah aggressively uses social assistance programs to garner support and to challenge its political opponents. Hezbollah often attempts to portray itself externally as an agent of Lebanese nationalism and as an example of a successful Shia political and military power to inspire other Shia populations like the Bahrainis, Saudis, Iraqis and Shia Yemenis.

Infrastructure

Hamas and Hezbollah are hindered by a lack of infrastructure much of which was recently damaged by the Israelis. But each group still uses available infrastructure to its strategic and tactical advantage, investing significantly to provide essential services of sewerage, water, trash removal, etc.

Gaza has suffered severe infrastructure damage from both the economic blockade and the conflict with Israel. Gaza is a densely packed urban area in which many neighborhoods were severely damaged by massive Israel Air Force (IAF) air strikes. Despite infrastructure shortfalls, the population does have access to both communication and transportation networks, and Gazans who can afford them maintain electrical generators.

Gaza has more cellular telephone subscribers than landline users which renders Hamas (and the populace) vulnerable to eavesdropping, jamming or spoofing. Information is broadcast over several Gazan radio and television stations and Hamas operates its own *al-Aqsa* TV station. When there is electrical power an estimated 70% of Gazans have access to TV and radios and 20% of the population owns a personal computer.[53] The internet is a growing source of information and communication, with current usage topping 300,000.[54]

Hamas' efforts to rebuild infrastructure have focused almost exclusively on the tunnels—used for smuggling operations—as this is the primary moneymaking source for Hamas and the primary means to resupply munitions and cash. Before the conflict as many as 8,000 smugglers worked on over 800 tunnels.[55] This system of tunnels was a key target for the Israeli military, but many remained open during the conflict and more have since been reopened. Hamas continues to smuggle in weapons and ammunitions in addition to food, cash supplies and even animals through this elaborate underground system.

Hezbollah also operates in infrastructure weakened by recent conflict, but the damage was less severe and not as concentrated as that in the Gaza Strip. Much of the infrastructure damage in Lebanon occurred in and around Beirut. Lebanon's infrastructure offers more reliability and options. Fiber optic communication lines, cellular telephone coverage and radio/TV broadcasts are widespread. Like Hamas, Hezbollah has its own television station, *al-Manar*, used for regional and international propaganda purposes. Hezbollah has access to a more-capable civilian infrastructure than Hamas, which allows better C^2, logistical and transportation options. Throughout its war with Israel, Hezbollah maintained essentially unfettered logistical connectivity to Syria and Turkey.

Hezbollah is following a pattern of co-opting what infrastructure it cannot control outright. For example it will soon control security at Beirut International Airport, thus allowing it to search, confiscate, secrete, or veto material that flies into Beirut. This has created for all intents and purposes, an Iranian airhead in the theater while allowing unfettered ability of Hamas leaders to travel or bypass trade sanctions. Where it is unable to co-opt, wherever possible, Hamas attempts to establish parallel infrastructure, especially as it relates to C^2.

In their respective conflicts with Israel, Hezbollah's better communications infrastructure gave it C^2 redundancy, and the ability to maintain effective communications throughout its battle. By contrast, Hamas suffered more outages and was therefore restricted to communication through messengers, which allowed Israel to "shape" the battlefield and take the tactical advantage.

Information

Hezbollah and Hamas recognize the importance of controlling and restricting information in building support, spreading propaganda and conducting information operations. The information infrastructure of the Gaza Strip, as mentioned above, affords Hamas the capabilities for communications and information operation activities. Telephone and internet are available to those seeking such access. Hamas' *al-Aqsa* television was bombed during the Israeli conflict and taken off the air briefly, but was able to resume broadcasting quickly. Hamas, like Hezbollah, uses such outlets to spread its perspective of the events and maintain the integrity of the IO message.

Like Hezbollah, Hamas understands the value of information and controlling the message, using deceptive photographic manipulation and other means to shape the narrative. Hamas is active in an "aggressive international and domestic information warfare campaign that seeks to present itself as the victim of Israeli oppression."[56] Fittingly, while Hamas seeks to portray itself as the weak victim, Hezbollah portrays itself as a strong and justified opponent.

Specialized publications—both print and internet based—stress Hamas' goal to create a Palestinian state and the destruction of Israel and create the IO message of political victimhood. Hamas is aggressively distributing its message via internet sites which disseminate official group statements as well as manipulated videos and pictures for propaganda purposes. Such propaganda has included staged scenes of civilian casualties and "re-edited" videos over-stating or even falsely portraying levels of destruction. Some evidence suggests that Hamas has even attempted to "block first aid and first responders to its own people until their suffering can be exploited for information warfare gains."[57] Hamas' perception management, while often clumsy, is engaged at the smaller (platoon/squad) sized elements. Unlike Western forces, the individual Hamas fighters are sensitized to the value of IO. Thus, by sheer volume, Hamas is able to overwhelm western media's poor analytic filter, successfully controlling the information environment.

Some analysts view Hamas' information campaign as unsuccessful—particularly when compared to Hezbollah. "Unlike Hizbullah [sic] who mastered the information campaign in its war with Israel in 2006, Hamas floundered," one source determined. While Hizbullah [sic] provided detailed accounts of how its guerillas were fighting the IDF, Hamas leaders cited verses from the Quran."[58] Nevertheless, Hamas is a force in the information arena and will continue to develop its skills in perception management and media manipulation with a continuing special focus on western media perception management. In terms of information infrastructure, Lebanon affords Hezbollah the same advantages it offers with other areas of the OE. Hezbollah has better information and communication options than Hamas, and uses them effectively.

Physical Environment

Hamas is limited to a much greater degree by its physical environment than Hezbollah—once again giving Hezbollah an advantage. The physical environment of Gaza consists mainly of flat-to-rolling terrain bordering the Mediterranean Sea between Egypt and Israel. Gaza is 139 square miles in size, slightly more than twice the size of Washington, DC.[59] Gaza's dry, flat costal plain is a small and highly urbanized dense environment.[60] One of the most important physical environment dimensions is that Gaza is almost completely surrounded by Israel.

In contrast, Lebanon is geographically larger with less densely populated urban centers. Lebanon also has a much wider range of terrain types (hills, mountains, and rock and brush covered terrain) as well as costal access. The complex and varied terrain of Lebanon provides excellent defensive cover to Hezbollah fighters and channelizes maneuver elements into historical paths—an often-overwhelming defensive advantage. Hamas is limited to the use of urban areas for defensive cover and concealment, but Lebanon's physical environment gives Hezbollah an advantage in concealing personnel and weapons.[61] The physical environment of Gaza can be more easily isolated and contained as opposed to the terrain of Lebanon. Hamas has neither strategic depth or resupply capabilities.[62]

Both groups have successfully constructed networks of underground tunnels. IDF sources estimate that prior to the recent conflict, Hamas had established hundreds of tunnels leading into Gaza from the Sinai.[63] As mentioned earlier, tunnels are used for smuggling and supply operations, tactical movement and force protection. Hezbollah has also developed a sophisticated network of tunnels, bunkers and caches across Lebanon.

Hamas makes the most of its defenses on Gaza's coastal and crowded urban terrain, however. Dense urbanization restricts movement and maneuverability of the mechanized Israelis while providing cover and concealment to Hamas fighters. Hamas, much like Hezbollah, prefers to hide and fight among the civilian population, using civilians as protection against overwhelming Israeli firepower and intelligence, surveillance, and reconnaissance (ISR) assets. Mosques, schools, hospitals and private homes have all been used as weapon storage sites, fighting positions and communication centers. Indeed, such facilities are often used as bait for Israeli kinetic action, and the resulting carnage documented and broadcasted for Hamas and Hezbollah IO benefit.

An important physical aspect of Gaza is the eight UN-sponsored refugee camps scattered across the strip. Hamas uses the tangled maze of these camps to its advantage and is familiar with each camp's ad-hoc architecture and underground layout. Camps in Gaza have extended underground components—networks of bunkers and control rooms—that can be used to move fighters, weapons, supplies and hostages. Reports indicate that many of the camps are connected by the elaborate tunnel system with hidden walkways and trap doors.[64] Israeli architect Eyal Weizman suggests that "Hamas has disappeared underground and Israel controls the sky, the more dominance they have to sky, the more the Palestinians master the subterranean."[65]

Hezbollah's wider range of terrain types provides the benefit of more tactical options and better defensive cover. Broken, rocky hills and tree-covered areas provide excellent natural hiding positions. Hezbollah also has access to sophisticated network of caches and bunkers, which helped it withstand Israeli attacks. Much of the conflict played out in the towns and small cities dotting the southern countryside, such as Marun ar-Rus and Bint Jbeil. Such terrain allowed Hezbollah to construct excellent defensive positions which Israel had trouble locating and thus effectively targeting. This terrain of southern Lebanon also restricts maneuver, channeling vehicles toward roads and other easily defended avenues of approach. These channels of movement bogged the Israelis down in the kind of attrition-based struggle that they are least optimized to fight.

Time

Both groups use time as a weapon against their enemies, particularly Israel and the United States. When looking to Israel and its goals, Hamas and Hezbollah each take a long-term view of time, feeling that a final victory over Israel is preordained and requires patience and prolonged commitment. Each group is willing to slowly grow its force while preparing for this long-term battle with the enemy. Both understand Western democracies' aversion to attrition to the point of unwillingness to suffer, or even inflict, casualties.

Both Hezbollah and Hamas will seek to use strategic and operational tempo against their enemies knowing that they will be less willing to prolong an engagement. Both favor delaying strategies, which give the organizations time to sway world opinion to their causes. This is a significant trait that must be understood by US Army planners when evaluating courses of action or scenarios against Islamic Resistance forces as quick victories will turn into costly occupation and prolonged battles of attrition.

By exploring the variables of each belligerent's OE, it is easier to understand the similarities and differences in the way in which each fought against Israel. Using this framework allows any comparative conclusion to better represent the subtleties of each group's actions. Without such understanding, any analysis would lack the context from which to fully draw lessons learned.

The 2006 Second Lebanon War

The 2006 conflict was triggered by successive Hezbollah attempts to kidnap Israeli soldiers for use as hostages or bartered in exchanges for terrorists held in Israel. It had made several previous attempts to kidnap IDF soldiers when its fifth attempt, on 12 July 2006, succeeded.[66] Under covering fire, including ATGMs, a Hezbollah team crossed into Israel and snatched two IDF soldiers, then exfiltrated back to Lebanese territory. Within days, Israeli Prime Minister Ehud Olmert declared the Hezbollah abduction an act of war and the stage was set for the 34-day long conflict between Hezbollah and Israel.

Hezbollah's strategy in the conflict was simple; it would focus strategically and operationally on continuing its rocket fire into Israel and attempt to weaken Israeli resolve while defending from its well-prepared positions in southern Lebanon. This supports Hezbollah's IO message that victory comes from the willingness to stand and fight a dominant opponent. This message has great currency in the Arab and Muslim world. Knowing Israel's sensitivity toward casualties, Hezbollah's Islamic Resistance would attempt to attrit Israeli forces as they advanced across southern Lebanon. Hezbollah used a combined-arms approach against the IDF and Israeli populace as well as the world audience to leverage its strengths.

Israel's response was initially focused on air strikes by the Israeli Air Force (IAF) with ground forces added to the mix toward the end of the conflict. Israel suffered 119 soldiers and 43 civilians killed and an estimated 300,000 (a staggering 20%) of its residents were displaced during the conflict.[67] In the end, a total of 4,000 rockets rained on Israel, resulting in one-third of the population being exposed to the terrifying rocket attacks.[68] Hezbollah claims that it lost 250 fighters killed while Israeli estimates indicate the number maybe closer to 600.[69] Ultimately, many analysts have concluded that Hezbollah was successful in turning the conflict into a loss for Israel even though there were no decisive battles, no clear winners and no clear losers. While Hezbollah claimed victory, Israel began to analyze its mistakes.[70]

Hezbollah TTPs

A review of past Hezbollah TTPs shows that the group—like Hamas—has conducted a range of attacks. These include indirect fire attacks, primarily with rocket and mortar; direct fire attacks (anti-armor and surface-to-air fire), employed explosives, IEDs/explosively-formed penetrator (EFP) and mines, and conducted raids, ambushes and kidnappings. Despite its lack of air power and armor, Hezbollah engaged Israeli forces in a major combat operation. In the 34-day war, Hezbollah fought in small, dispersed and shielded units utilizing "hit-and-run" tactics that denied IAF targets and limited Israel's ISR effectiveness.

Unlike Hamas, which suffered C^2 decapitation and degradation on the first day from massive Israeli air strikes, Hezbollah did not suffer such an overwhelmingly devastating attack. Israeli targeting in Lebanon focused on Lebanese civilian infrastructure, such radio and television stations and airports, rather than Hezbollah infrastructure. According to one Israeli commentator, the most important lesson that Israel learned during its Hezbollah conflict was that, "in the face of enemies who have opted for a strategy of attrition and attacking from a distance, Israel will present itself as a 'crazy country', the kind that will respond in a massive and unfettered assault, with no proportion to the amount of casualties it has endured."[71]

Hezbollah was very successful in cover and concealment, preparation of its fighting positions, and its coordination of direct fire support.[72] However, despite such success, mistakes were made. Hezbollah deficiencies include controlling maneuver forces, integrating indirect fire and movement and small arms marksmanship. To put this into historical perspective, despite Hezbollah's weaknesses, it scored more "Israeli causalities per Arab fighter in 2006 than did any of Israel's state opponents in 1956, 1967, 1973, or the 1982 Arab-Israeli interstate wars."[73] And it forced Israel to rethink its doctrine and strategy.

Operational Shielding

Both Hezbollah and Hamas understand the value of operational shielding. Both groups utilize "hugging" or hiding tactics designed to force Israel to abstain from attacking due to fears of collateral causalities. Hezbollah and Hamas fighters tried to blend in with the civilian populations and use residential structures for firing positions and hide-outs. For example, Hamas fighters sought shelter in diplomatic facilities (consulates, residences and UN buildings), while Hezbollah's leader Hassan Nasrallah is thought to have commanded the Second Lebanon War from the Iranian Embassy in Beirut.[74] Videotapes show Hezbollah placed rocket launchers in firing positions next to residential buildings or hidden inside garages between fire missions.[75]

Rocket launchers were also dispersed into urban settings to maximize operational shielding. The Israeli counter-fire missions were limited due to the fear of increasing civilian causalities. Hezbollah's ability to "exploit virtually any built up area and familiar terrain as fortresses or ambush sites at least partially compensated for IDF armor, air mobility, superior firepower, and sensors."[76] Hezbollah used civilians as human shields and civilian homes to conceal launchers and as direct fire combat positions. Hezbollah also fired rocket launchers from within buildings and homes.[77]

Hezbollah fighters blended in with the population effectively. Some did use civilian clothing for deception; however, many wore military uniforms.[78] There are even examples of IDF soldiers hesitating to fire on Hezbollah fighters "because their kit, from a distance, looked so much like the IDF infantry's."[79]

Defense

Hezbollah combat engineers constructed excellent defensive positions. Numerous strong points were dispersed across the towns of southern Lebanon. Outposts were constructed in rural areas for security and intelligence operations. The IDF reported finding over 500 weapon caches and hundreds of mobile rocket/missile sites across this well-defended area.[80] This dispersed-yet-integrated defense was composed of primarily company-size strong points (including primary, secondary and decoy positions). Hezbollah was well prepared to fight IDF units. David Makovsky and Jeffery White posit that "Nasrallah apparently planned to deter Israel from deep attacks into Lebanon with his rocket forces and limit and exhaust any Israeli ground operations with his defensive systems in the south, which was based on ATGMs and well-hidden and protected fighters."[81]

Hezbollah built launch sites for both its short-range and medium-range rockets throughout southern Lebanon. Many of these were built into the ground, using pneumatic lifts to raise and lower the launchers from underground shelters. Many were launched from trucks positioned as stand-alone launchers. Firing teams sought protection in nearby bunkers and caves to hide from IDF counter-battery attacks.[82]

Hezbollah often participated in extended direct firefights with the IDF. One excellent example is the fight at outpost Shaked. At this location, a "dug-in Hezbollah defensive position remained in place on a critical hillcrest near the Israeli border between Avivim and Marun ar Ras, exchanging fire with IDF tanks and infantry for more than 12 hours before finally being destroyed in place by Israeli fire."[83]

Again at Marun ar Ras, Hezbollah defenders fought room-to-room with IDF soldiers holding their positions for close to 7 hours; at Bint Jbeil, Hezbollah fighters battled IDF units for 4 days after which the IDF forces retrograded and executed bombing strikes. Clearly, these cases—and numerous others not cited—show that Hezbollah has the capability to sustain the close-in, direct-fire fight. Hezbollah also succeeded in conducting counterattacks against the IDF at the platoon level or smaller, although examples of this are less common.[84] In situations where IDF units were able to clear Hezbollah fighters from their defensive positions, they infiltrated back and quickly reestablished their positions once the IDF units moved on or withdrew.

Maneuver

Hezbollah showed that it possessed the ability to tactically maneuver under fire and, unlike Hamas, hold ground while conducting limited maneuver operations.[85] Hezbollah gave Israel a substantial infantry and anti-armor fight and showed skills in tactically hiding, moving and dispersing. Hamas fighters, in contrast, instead often ran to hide in tunnels and buildings. Limited examples exist of Hamas standing its ground against IDF fires.

Fires

Hezbollah was able to maintain a steady stream of Katyusha rockets throughout the entire conflict. Both Hezbollah and Hamas used rockets as their primary strategic and operational fires response to the IDF. Hezbollah's rockets represented excellent "psychological and political weapons with strategic affect."[86] Hezbollah launched close to 4,000 rockets with more than 200 rockets per day fired into Israel during the final days of the war.[87]

As noted, Hezbollah's rocket inventory included the long-range Iranian-made Zelzal -2, Nazeat, Fajr-3, and the Fajr-5, but the significant majority (80-90%) of its rocket inventory consisted of the shorter-range, proven Katyusha rockets.[88] Whether or not Hezbollah possessed the capability to adjust the fire of these area-fire weapons is academic as the vast majority simply rained down on Israeli citizens.

Perhaps the most important difference between Hezbollah and Hamas' artillery capability was in the ability to integrate fires. Hezbollah successfully integrated anti-armor fires with indirect fires, providing cover for reposition and subsequent anti-armor engagements.[89] Hezbollah was also able to successfully separate and isolate Israeli infantry and supporting armor units. Hamas, however, has not demonstrated such capabilities.

In addition, Hezbollah surprised Israeli forces with a new strike capability—the C-802 anti-ship missile. On July 14, 2006 Hezbollah fired two of these missiles at the INS *Hanit*, causing significant damage.[90] Hezbollah leaders coupled this surprise attack capability with sophisticated media exploitation. Moments prior to the strike, Nasrallah went on *al-Manar* TV and provided a live countdown to the strike. As the missile was launched, he confidently suggested that viewers in Beirut look toward the west for a spectacular sight. The timing of the broadcast was impeccable and serving as a lethal theatrical drum roll. This is an excellent example of Hezbollah's ability to use its media and information prowess as a combat multiplier as well as highlighting its flair for the dramatic that results in a massive IO victory.

In the direct-fire close fighting Hezbollah employed ATGMs by anti-armor teams of 5-6 fighters. Typically the teams allowed IDF tanks to pass by and then engaged them from the rear. Hezbollah fighters fired ATGMs at buildings that IDF soldiers had used to shelter from small-arms and mortar fire. These tandem-warhead missiles either penetrated deeply into the buildings' interiors or collapsed them.[91] Although very few Israeli tanks suffered a catastrophic ATGM hit, many IDF tanks were damage and taken out of action.[92]

Hezbollah's ATGM armory could boast of advanced missiles like the AT-14E Kornet missile, which reportedly "took a considerable toll on Israeli armor in the confused, sporadic ground war that raged close to the border."[93] Hezbollah also employed the RPG 29, the AT-4 Spigot, the AT-5 Spandrel, and the AT-13 METIS-M. Final estimates indicate that 40 tanks were damaged, "resulting in the deaths of 30 tank crewmen—25 percent of the IDF's entire combat losses in the war."[94] These losses, especially with regard to the sophisticated Israeli Merkava tank, constituted another Hezbollah IO victory.

IEDs/ Mines

Hezbollah used IEDs and land mines across southern Lebanon. "Explosive pits" and EFPs were emplaced along main roads in southern Lebanon. Coupled with rocket attacks, this ordinance limited the IDF's ability to maneuver. In addition, according to a Strategic Studies Institute's report, "Hezbollah's minefield employment was sometimes tied into direct fire defensive systems in a systematic way and sometimes not."[95] However, there are examples of the use of mines coupled with "obstacles overwatched by fires," evidence of Hezbollah's sophistication.[96]

C^2/Intelligence

Hezbollah's C^2 can be characterized as centralized planning and decentralized tactical execution. A CSIS report states "Hezbollah acted as a 'distributed network' of small cells and units acting with considerable independence, and capable of rapidly adapting to local conditions rather than having to react faster than the IDF's decision cycle, they could largely ignore it, waiting out Israeli attacks, staying in positions, reinfiltrating or reemerging from cover, and choosing the time to attack or ambush."[97]

An additional Hezbollah strength was its ability to maintain communications throughout the conflict, while intercepting and exploiting Israeli communications. "Hezbollah's ability to listen to, and locate, cell phone traffic had been a major problem [for Israel] in the fighting with Hezbollah."[98] The quality of Hezbollah's information infrastructure—including the redundancy of communications options—made C^2 much easier for Hezbollah than Hamas' situation two years later. Hezbollah's excellent, diverse, and hard-to-target C^2 capabilities included fiber-optic landlines, cell phones, secure radio, messengers, the internet and the *al-Manar* television station.[99] Without such effective C^2, Hezbollah's "fighting and rocket attacks would have degenerated into small local fights and haphazard rocket firing,[100] much like Hamas experienced two years later.

Information Operations

Hezbollah controlled the information environment and integrated kinetic operations into its strategic IO. The organization has conducted some of the most successful information operations in the Middle East by employing many experts specializing in psychological warfare and propaganda, operating its own television, radio, and internet sites and collaborating with supporting media (such as that owned by like-minded Islamists). Hezbollah focused on stressing Israeli vulnerabilities, while highlighting Hezbollah's battlefield successes and Lebanese civilian casualties and infrastructure damage. Hezbollah accomplished this by performing sophisticated editing and photo and video manipulation, presenting a skewed picture of the war's progress.[101]

Media exploitation was one of Hezbollah's most effective weapons. According to one source, Hezbollah's IO motto could be summed up as, "if you haven't captured it on film—you haven't fought."[102] Ultimately, all of Hezbollah's battlefield successes integrated into its overall IO plan—its greatest victory of the war being the destruction of the myth of Israel's battlefield invincibility. In the end, Hezbollah survived, and gained increased international and regional recognition of its military capabilities and warfighting skills. Hamas would not fare as well.

A cursory review of these conflicts shows Hezbollah is capable of tactical actions that are much more complex than a typical non-state belligerent. They show sophistication and the clear ability to conduct major combat operations. Hezbollah's use of effective TTPs, mastery of the terrain and ability to simultaneously negate Israel's advantages (mobility and air supremacy) proved more successful and gave Israel a surprisingly harder fight with strategic consequences. As the next section will show, Hamas has learned much from Hezbollah, through Hezbollah-sponsored training, weapons assistance, and adoption of similar TTPs. Despite this cooperation and mentorship, Hamas has to this point in time been unable to match Hezbollah's successful tactical actions.

2008-2009 Hamas/Israeli Conflict

In April 2008, the IDF declared a significant and increasing threat from Hamas after months of receiving rocket and mortar fire from the Gaza Strip. An Israeli statement claimed that threats from Hamas "include improved capabilities to carry out complex terrorist attacks such as mass-casualty attacks and the abduction of soldiers and civilians; an increase in the scope, accuracy, range and force of rocket fire into Israel and increasing the threat of anti-tank weapons to Israel's tanks and armored vehicles and to IDF soldiers."[103] Two months later, following a period of growing tension, Israel and Hamas established a six-month truce, mandating that Hamas cease rocket fire against Israel and Israel end its economic blockade on Gaza. Neither Hamas nor the Israelis completely honored this cease-fire; rocket fire did not stop and the supplies into Gaza were not adequate to pull Gaza out of its growing economic and humanitarian crises. In December 2008 both parties failed to agree on conditions to extend the truce and the Hamas/Israeli conflict ignited on 19 December 2008.

The conflict, known as Operation CAST LEAD to the Israelis, began with a massive Israeli air strike against Hamas high-value targets (HVTs) across the Gaza Strip. Operation CAST LEAD, which was intended to stop the harassing Hamas rocket attacks on Israel, lasted more than three weeks. In the end, Hamas estimates, more than 4,000 homes were destroyed and 17,000 others damaged during the campaign,[104] with recent estimates indicating that 1,417 people (including 255 police officers and 236 Hamas fighters) were killed.[105]

The Israeli perception was that Hamas was taken by surprise.[106] However, two days prior to the air strike, senior Hamas leaders were reportedly moving into hiding, and key Hamas materials and computers were being moved to different locations. Hamas fighters left their bases, and according to an International Crisis Group observation, police forces chose to "operate outside of their stations for the sake of self-protection at night, when IDF attacks were most likely."[107] Israel may have surprised Hamas with the scope of its initial air attack, but Hamas was clearly preparing for some type of Israeli action. Perhaps, as a CSIS report suggests, "like the Hezbollah's leader in 2006, Hamas fundamentally mischaracterized its enemy in terms of both its intentions and military capabilities."[108]

Prior to the conflict, a Qassam Brigade spokesman said Hamas was confident in its ability to conduct both offensive and defensive operations against the IDF. "Our defense plan is based, to a great extent, on rockets which have not yet been used and on a network of ditches and tunnels dug under a large area of the Strip. The [Israeli] army will be surprised when it sees fighters coming up out of the ground and engaging it with unexpected equipment and weapons."[109] Those capabilities, if not overstated, were greatly underutilized—resulting in Hamas failing to achieve its goals against Israeli forces.

Hamas TTPs

Reviews of past Hamas actions show that the group is capable of conducting a wide variety of attacks including indirect and direct fire attacks, raids, ambushes/kidnappings and the employment of IEDs/mines. In terms of defending Gaza against Israel, Hamas apparently wanted to "wage a guerilla war of attrition, especially in densely populated built-up areas"[110]—a strategy drawing almost exclusively from the Hezbollah 2006 game plan. The tactical plan was to draw Israel deep into Gaza and attack IDF units with small-arms and ATGM fire. If successful, Hamas would draw IDF units into killing zones and inflict significant causalities, eroding Israel's willingness to continue the fight. At the operational level, Hamas planned to use rocket and mortar attacks as a show of force and continue to harass the population of Israel.

Again, pulling from lessons learned in the 2006 conflict, Hamas obviously attempted to use many of Hezbollah's common TTPs. These included rocket attacks to inflict politically unacceptable Israeli casualties, "hit-and-run" direct engagement attacks followed by dispersion into small units, and fighting from inside civilian structures with the ultimate aim of executing their attrition strategy.

IDF Commander Colonel Halevy claimed that Hamas' forces were divided into six territorial brigades (operating in the four sectors previously mentioned), each tasked with defending a specific sector of Gaza. There are indications that the majority of the brigades were composed largely of local fighters. Each brigade consisted of three battalions, which were organized into company and platoons,[111] composed by the core group of fighters supplemented with local manpower, as previously discussed.

Operational Shielding

Hamas used the urban terrain to its advantage in terms of providing cover and operational and tactical shielding. It placed fighters and weapon caches inside schools, mosques, and other public buildings in addition to homes. In preparation, Hamas booby-trapped houses and buildings, placed IEDs in homes, and used its tunnel network to move and resupply, albeit not as effectively as Hezbollah. Hamas used Gaza's main hospital as a command center and defensive fighting position.[112]

Defense

Hamas used the Hezbollah model and built up defensive positions in urban areas—and, as one report states, Hamas promised to turn Gaza "into a graveyard for Israeli forces." It boldly announced that "the Zionist enemy will see surprises and will regret carrying out such an operation and will pay a heavy price."[113]

Hamas fighters, however, were unable to achieve the majority of their defensive goals; many Hamas fighters simply fled, or hid, while others were killed by effective Israeli fires. The one success was its ability to continue to fire rockets at Israel throughout the operation, although Israel degraded this capability by suppressing or overrunning the launch sites. At the beginning of the conflict, Hamas launched up to 80 rockets each day, but that number was reduced to no more than 20 at the end. In contrast, Hezbollah fired more than 200 rockets per day throughout its Israeli conflict.[114]

Maneuver

Some close combat fighting did occur, but "sustained ground fighting was limited, and Hamas protected itself by avoiding direct engagements."[115] Like

Hezbollah, Hamas favored "hit-and-run" tactics, dispersing quickly to avoid IDF counterattacks. The IDF, though, was able to move quickly, use urban cover and conduct "suppressive fire to deny Hamas the ability to repeat the kind of successful short range strikes and swarming of multiple firing of such weapons that Hezbollah had carried out in 2006."[116] Hamas' defenses appear to have folded and the fighters quickly dispersed back into the civilian population. The strategy to draw the Israelis deep into Gaza and attack with strong resistance had failed.[117] As discussed earlier, IDF soldiers were surprised by this lack of resistance and the overall low quality of the Hamas fighters in contrast to the performances of the "village fighters" of Hezbollah.[118]

Fires

Hamas typically relied upon indirect rocket attacks and small arms fire. Overall, Hamas failed to surprise the IDF with either its weaponry or tactics. There were no incidents like Hezbollah's surprise use of the C-802 anti-ship missile during the Hamas conflict. There was one report of an ATGM being used, but no information has been provided on its effectiveness. Reports also show that RPG-29s were used several times—with one penetrating an armored Israeli bulldozer. The IAF also reports that Hamas fired anti-aircraft missiles at it—probably the SA-7.[119]

Given Hamas' stated goal of acquiring advanced ATGMs as part of its overall military build-up, why was there so little use of this capability? It was most likely a function of poorly trained and disciplined ATGMs gunners and lack of necessary cueing systems for targeting and effective IDF tactics (use of smoke, bypassing Hamas defensive positions, and maneuver at night). IDF troops surrounded and drove Hamas from many of its rocket-firing positions and into Gaza City, where the IDF was able to effectively eliminate much of the tactical threat with counterfire. IDF forces also destroyed many of Hamas' stockpiles and safe houses in earlier air strikes. As more information becomes available on Hamas' actions during this operation, more definitive analysis can be presented as to why options were or were not used. It simply may have been a choice Hamas leaders made to preserve their capabilities for another battle.

IEDs/ Mines

Hamas placed IEDs on most key streets and main intersections—even planting IEDs in satellite dishes at residential sites to be remotely detonated once IDF soldiers approached.[120] IDF units reported finding caches of weapons—including large amounts of ammunition—in most of the buildings it searched in Gaza City. This prepositioning of weapons and supplies gave the Hamas fighters the ability to fire from one building, leave the weapons behind, walk the streets as a civilian, and then enter another building start fighting again.[121] Hamas planned to rely on its substantial stockpiles of rockets, small-arms and IEDs to deter and counter Israeli actions. However, IDF units were able to bypassed Hamas strong points and negate many of the IEDs and booby trapped buildings based upon excellent Israeli intelligence. One-third of all Gaza homes encountered by the IDF were booby-trapped.[122]

C^2/Intelligence

Early assessments show that Hamas struggled with its C^2 and some reports indicate that IAF strikes destroyed Hamas telecommunications facilities in Gaza.[123] Additionally, Hamas' cell phone network was degraded. As a result, Hamas commanders were forced to "cease most of their communication with field units," relying on messengers or walkie-talkies. A CSIS report supports the claim that IAF strikes significantly degraded Hamas command structure and communication capabilities.[124]

Fighters tended to avoid direct engagements with the IDF and many chose not to fight. There is very limited reporting of aggressive Hamas coordinated direct actions. Only one report from *BBC* sources claimed that Hamas fighters ambushed and aggressively attacked IDF units during the early stages of its advance into Gaza City.[125] Most reports asserted that Hamas tended to operate as fixed defensive units "with only 300 fighters" actually fighting against the IDF.[126]

Israel assessed that Hamas' C^2 capabilities were weak and ineffective and speculated that some of the rockets fired by Hamas post cease-fire were "only fired because of a breakdown in Hamas' C^3 capabilities."[127] In addition, Israeli intelligence collection efforts were aided by the poor "communication discipline" of Hamas.[128] It appears that superior Israeli intelligence/IPB (assisted greatly by Fatah informants) and an inferior Hamas C^2 system caused delays in command decisions and its fighters' actions.

Information Operations

Hamas also knows the value of IO campaigns, but its means and target audiences are significantly different. As stated earlier, Hamas' IO message attempts to portray the organization as the victim of overwhelming and unjustified Israeli actions. Hamas conducted a successful and integrated IO campaign utilizing a spectrum of tools including radio, TV, internet and, importantly, fighters at all echelons trained on the importance of IO—constantly scanning for exploitable opportunities. While Hezbollah focused on the Arab and Muslim world as its target audience, Hamas targeted a more Western audience, with the overall goal of pressuring Israel to "stop the killing." Unlike the 2006 conflict, Israel was more sanitized and proactive in its response to Hamas IO messages and denial of information outlets to Hamas. For example, Israel did not allow foreign reporters access to Gaza, jammed and kinetically targeted Hamas media outlets and promoted the Israeli narrative via outlets such as YouTube.com. YouTube messages were specifically targeted to US audiences, using IDF personnel speaking American English. In response to these Israeli initiatives, Hamas countered by courting sympathetic international groups and organizations especially in Europe.

This begs the question: were Hamas' military capabilities and skills overblown, or was Hamas simply challenged by a superior force? There is no single answer. Undoubtedly, Israel learned valuable lessons from its 2006 engagement with Hezbollah and applied those lessons against Hamas. Clearly, the Israelis feel that their tactical maneuvers and early devastating air strikes effectively paralyzed Hamas forces, allowing them to control the fight. Just as important, Israeli operational thinking clearly stresses avoidance of the attrition battle. To this end, Israeli forces moved quickly to their objectives, bypassing Hamas resistance. Additionally, Hamas' capabilities were not as robust as originally thought. For example, clearly Hamas lacked the advanced skills—such as signal intelligence (SIGINT)—that enabled Hezbollah. While Hamas retains the ability to conduct suicide bombings and rocket attacks, this is a smaller order of magnitude than conventionally fighting an opponent like the IDF. Hamas' critical deficiencies in training, basic combat skills, intelligence, resupply and overall C^2 have all been highlighted and will require significant time and resources to correct.

Not surprisingly, Hamas took a different view of its performance—one based on classic Arabic thinking that victory belongs to the smaller force that survives against a superior military power. Yet, despite this early celebration, there is clear evidence that Hamas recognizes its flaws. In late January 2009, reports begin to surface that Hamas was conducting an internal review of its less-than-stellar performance. Additional reporting indicates that the Qassam Brigades and Hamas intelligence units have admitted shortcomings and are reviewing their actions.[129] Anthony Cordesman concludes that "Hamas commanders seem to have felt that their defense tactics and use of IEDs had been far less successful than they anticipated . . . that their defensive plans did not make effective use of buildings and terrain in many cases . . . and that homemade explosives failed more often than expected, and that Hamas forces had unanticipated difficulties in resupply."[130]

In the end, Hamas performed poorly and was forced to accept a less-than-satisfactory ceasefire. Unlike Hezbollah, Hamas cannot claim any significant success in its fight against Israel. As one CSIS report concludes, "the end result was that Hamas initiated the conflict as a weak non-state belligerent that could launch rocket and mortar attacks on Israeli civilian and civil facilities over an extended period of time but had little other warfighting capability other than using its own densely populated urban areas as barriers. It did so in part because it had no other real means of combat."[131] And despite losses of equipment, supporting infrastructure and fighters, there is "little doubt that Hamas, like Hezbollah, will rise from the rubble to emerge as strong as ever and probably stronger."[132]

Conclusion

While important lessons can be gained in any comparison of conflicts and forces in those conflicts, one must be careful not to draw them too quickly and too broadly. Looking at a belligerent through the lens of its unique OE allows for better analytical context of both the operation and belligerent. In the specific case of Israel and its enemies, the belligerents' responses to Israel's ground offensive were different—reflecting their OE, as well as their overall capabilities and level of sophistication. Israel, like many in the West, may have assumed that Hamas would present a Hezbollah-like fight, but such assumptions can be faulty, misleading and potentially dangerous. According to a Washington Institute for Near East Policy analyst, "It is always a mistake to lump these two movements together. Hezbollah deserves the title 'Islamic Resistance' as it actually fought battles of maneuver and assaulted Israeli fortified lines, while 'the resistance of Hamas' has always been fiction."[133] In fact, Hezbollah fights such categorization and views itself as fiercely independent of Hamas. It is worth noting that Hezbollah did not get involved in the recent fight between Israel and Hamas—most likely because Hezbollah realized Hamas might not win and it did not want its hard-won 2006 victory tarnished.

Stephen Biddle and Jeffrey Friedman of the Strategic Studies Institute argue that "Hezbollah's skills in conventional warfighting were clearly imperfect in 2006—but they were also well within the observed bounds of other state military belligerents in the Middle East and elsewhere, and significantly superior to many such states."[134]

Overall, Hamas was not as well-armed and supplied as Hezbollah. Hamas was unable to offer any effective resistance to the ground fight, while Hezbollah offered substantial resistance to Israeli forces and conducted successful operations against the IDF. Both groups were successful at bringing the conflict directly to the Israeli population. And both conflicts help to reveal Iran's destabilizing role in the region and its increasing influence in the Arab world.

Hezbollah presented the Israelis with a well trained, well led and suitably equipped force with sufficient space to defend in depth. Hamas was inadequately trained and poorly led with little space to trade for producing Israeli casualties. In the case of the 2006 conflict, the Israelis underestimated the capabilities of Hezbollah and overestimated its capability to fight such an opponent. Such miscalculation is a recipe for international humiliation. Conversely, as in the case of Hamas, an underequipped, ill trained and poorly commanded opponent can be an annoyance—but it will not stand long against significant national power. Hamas presented the Israelis with a poor imitation of Hezbollah and Hezbollah wisely stayed on the sideline and watched the events unfold. Both actions reinforce—one positively and one negatively—the lesson that a well trained, disciplined and well equipped paramilitary force, can fight successfully against a national Army for a limited, possibly substantial, period of time.

NOTES

1. Tradoc Intelligence Support Activity (TRISA)–Threats, *The Contemporary Operational Environment*, (Fort Leavenworth, Kansas: Tradoc Intelligence Support Activity, July 2007) and further explained in Field Manual (FM) 3-0, *Operations*, para. 1-22.

2. FM 3-0, *Operations*, para. 5-29.

3. Aaron D. Pina, "Fatah and Hamas: the New Palestinian Factional Reality," *CRS Report for Congress*, 3 March 2006, 1.

4. Office of the Director of National Intelligence, "Annual Threat Assessment of the Intelligence Community for the House Permanent Select Committee on Intelligence," 25 Feb 2009.

5. Ibid., 8.

6. It is important to note that until 11 September 2001, Hezbollah had killed more Americans than any other terrorist organization. Key Hezbollah successes include the 1983 US Embassy and Marine barracks bombing in Beirut, the 1984 kidnapping of CIA officer Wm. Buckley, the 1985 hijacking of TWA Flight 847, the 1988 capture (and later murder) of USMC Col. Rich Higgins, the 1992 Israeli Embassy strikes in Argentina, the 1996 attack on Khobar Towers in Saudi Arabia and, most recently, the January 2007 attack on the Karbala government JCC compound in Iraq where several US Soldiers were abducted and later killed.

7. "Annual Threat Assessment of the Intelligence Community", 11.

8. Central Intelligence Agency, "CIA World Factbook–Gaza Strip," 10 Feb 2009, https://www.cia.gov/library/publications/the-world-factbook/print/gz.html.

9. Anthony H. Cordesman, "The 'Gaza War:' A Strategic Analysis," *Center For Strategic & International Studies*, http://www.csis.org/component/option,com_csis_pubs/task,view/id,5250/type,1/.

10. Col. Ronen Shviki, TRADOC IDF LNO, discussion with CSI study group, 23 Feb 09, Fort Leavenworth, Kansas.

11. "Hamas at the Crossroads," *Jane's Foreign Report*, 3 Feb 2009, http://www.janes.com/news/security/terrorism/fr/fr090203_1_n.shtml.

12. Ibid.

13. Matthew Levitt, "Political Hardball within Hamas: Hardline Militants Calling Shots in Gaza," *Policy Watch* #1450, 6 Jan 2009, The Washington Institute for Near East Policy, http://www.washingtoninstitute.org/templateC05.php?CID=2982

14. "Hamas at the Crossroads."

15. Levitt.

16. "Islamic Resistance (IR) Military Wing Hezbollah Lebanon," *(UNCLASSIFIED/FOUO) TRISA Handbook No. 16*, (Fort Leavenworth, Kansas: March 2007), 8.

17. "Politics of Hezbollah," *(UNCLASSIFIED/FOUO) TRISA Handbook No. 15*, (Fort Leavenworth, Kansas: February 2007), 18.

18. Intelligence and Terrorism Information Center, "Hamas's Military Buildup in the Gaza Strip," Israel Intelligence Heritage and Commemoration Center (IICC), April 2008, 4, http://www.terrorism-info.org.il/malam_multimedia/English/eng_n/pdf/hamas_080408.pdf.

19. Ibid.

20. Ibid., 16.

21. Cordesman, "The 'Gaza War:' A Strategic Analysis."

22. "Hamas–Military Wing," *(UNCLASSIFIED/FOUO)TRISA Handbook No. 27*, (Fort Leavenworth, Kansas: January 2007), 8.

23. Cordesman, "The 'Gaza War:' A Strategic Analysis."

24. Cordesman, "The 'Gaza War:' A Strategic Analysis."

25. Yoram Cohen and Matthew Levitt, "Hamas Arms Smuggling: Egypt's Challenge," *Policy Watch* #1484, 2 March 2009, The Washington Institute for Near East Policy, http://www.washingtoninstitute.org/pdf.php?template=C05&CID=3020.

26. Charles Levinson and Jay Solomon, "Israel Kills Hamas Security Chief, Hits UN Site," *Wall Street Journal*, 16 Jan 09, http://online.wsj.article/SB12320780663885189.html.

27. Amos Harel, "IDF: Hamas Men Beginning To Desert; Army Steps Up Gaza Op," *Haaretz.com*, 12 January 2009, http://www.haaretz.com/hasen/spages/1054245.html.

28. Cordesman, "The 'Gaza War:' A Strategic Analysis."

29. Kim Cragin, Peter Chalk, Sara Daly, Brian Jackson, *Sharing the Dragon's Teeth: Terrorist Groups and the Exchange of New Technologies*, (Santa Monica, California: RAND, 2007), http://www.rand.org/pubs/monographs/2007/RAND_MG485.pdf.

30. Anthony H. Cordesman, "Preliminary 'Lessons' of the Israeli- Hezbollah War," *Center For Strategic & International Studies*, 11 Sept 2006, 7, http://www.csis.org/%20id=?cx=006046696219301290917%3A23rjzx7mdwy&cof=FORID%3A11&q=Hezbollah&option=search#1074.

31. "Summer 2006 Lebanon War: Hezbollah and Israel," *(UNCLASSIFIED/FOUO)TRISA-Threats*, (Fort Leavenworth, Kansas), 6.

32. Ibid., 78.

33. Cordesman, "Preliminary 'Lessons' of the Israeli- Hezbollah War."

34. Cordesman, "Preliminary 'Lessons' of the Israeli- Hezbollah War."

35. Steven J. Zaloga, *Soviet Tanks and Combat Vehicles of World War Two* (London: Arms and Armour Press, 1984), 150–54. The term "Katyusha" has come to describe descendants of the Soviet WWII free-flight mass bombardment rocket called "Stalin's Organ" by German troops. Usually 122- or 132-mm in diameter, the six-foot long rockets weigh about 90 lbs including a warhead of about 48 lbs. The rocket has a solid propellant of tubular shape with a single central nozzle in the rear and stabilized by cruciform fins of pressed sheet steel. Because they were marked with the letter K, for Voronezh Komintern Factory, Red Army troops adopted the nickname from the

popular wartime song, "Katyusha" ("Katie"), about a girl longing for her absent man away on military service. Jeremy M. Sharp, "Israel-Hamas-Hezbollah: The Current Conflict," *CRS Report for Congress*, 21 July 2006, 9, http://www.law.umaryland.edu/marshall/crsreports/crsdocuments/RL33566_07212006.pdf.

36. There is some disagreement on the intent and accuracy of this bombardment, see Nicholas Noe, "A Response to Andrew Exum's 'Hizbollah at War: A Military Assessment,'" *Mideastwire.com*, 5, states: ". . . Hizbullah's use of rocket attacks on Israeli military targets—thus apparently buying hook, line and sinker the Israeli leaderships claim that the Katyusha was merely . . . a "psychological" weapon of terror wielded randomly on innocent civilians. The well-reported strikes on the intelligence facility at Meron in Northern Israel . . . [and] . . . Hizbullah's reported use of drones in its own targeting. Left out of the narrative as well is the issue of Hizbullah's ability to target chemical facilities in Haifa . . ."

37. *TRISA Handbook No. 16*, 27.

38. Jonathan Spyer, "Lebanon 2006: Unfinished War," *The Middle East Review of International Affairs* (March 2008), http://meria.idc.ac.il/journal/2008/issue1/jv12no1a1.asp.

39. "CIA World Factbook–Gaza Strip."

40. Tradoc Intelligence Support Activity (TRISA)–Threats, *Operational Environment Analysis: Gaza*, (Fort Leavenworth, Kansas: Tradoc Intelligence Support Activity. Currently in draft, soon to be published).

41. Matthew Levitt, "Hiding Terrorist Activity," Middle East Strategy at Harvard MESH Blog, posted 6 Jan 2009, http://blogs.law.harvard.edu/mesh/2009/01/hiding-terrorist-activity.

42. "Hamas," *Jane's World Insurgency and Terrorism*, 23 Sept 2008.

43. Matthew Levitt, "Countering Transnational Threats: Terrorism, Narco-Trafficking, and WMD Proliferation," *The Washington Institute for Near East Policy Policy Focus* #92, February 2009, http://www.washingtoninstitute.org/pubPDFs/PolicyFocus92.pdf.

44. Central Intelligence Agency, "CIA World Factbook–Lebanon," 5 March 2009, https://www.cia.gov/library/publications/the-world-factbook/geos/le.html.

45. Ibid.

46. *TRISA Handbook No. 16*, 10

47. "Hamas at the Crossroads."

48. TRISA-Threats, "Operational Environment Analysis: Gaza."

49. "CIA World Factbook–Gaza Strip."

50. Steven Erlanger, "A Gaza War Full of Traps and Trickery," *New York Times*, 11 Jan 2009, http://www.nytimes.com/2009/01/11/world/middleeast/11hamas.html.

51. "CIA World Factbook–Lebanon."

52. "CIA World Factbook–Lebanon."

53. TRISA-Threats, "Operational Environment Analysis: Gaza."

54. "CIA World Factbook–Gaza Strip."

55. TRISA–Threats, "Operational Environment Analysis: Gaza."

56. *TRISA Handbook No. 26*, 43.

57. *TRISA Handbook No. 27*, 60. Observations from video exploitation analysis of Hamas videos and http://www.jcpa.org.

58. "Hamas at the Crossroads."

59. "CIA World Factbook–Gaza Strip."

60. "CIA World Factbook–Gaza Strip."

61. Hampton Stephens, "The War in Gaza: Can Israel Have Military Success?" *World Politics Review*, 02 Jan 09, http://www.worldpoliticsreview.com.

62. "Ending the War in Gaza," *International Crisis Group Policy Briefing*, Middle East Briefing No. 26, 5 January 2009, http://www.crisisgroup.org/home/index.cfm?id=5838.

63. Cordesman, "The 'Gaza War:' A Strategic Analysis," 20.

64. Don Duncan, "Palestinian Militants' Advantage in Gaza?" *Christian Science Monitor*, 20 March 2009, http://www.csmonitor.com/2009/0320/p09s01-coop.html (accessed 20 March 2009).

65. Ibid.

66. Nicholas Blanford, "Deconstructing Hezbollah's Surprise Military Prowess," *Jane's Intelligence Review*, November 2006, 24.

67. Spyer.

68. David Makovsky and Jeffery White, "Lessons and Implications of the Israel–Hezbollah War," *Policy Focus* #60, October 2006, 7, The Washington Institute for Near East Policy, http://www.washingtoninstitute.org/pubPDFs/PolicyFocus60.pdf.

69. "Army Chief Says Israel May Have to Confront Hezbollah Attempts to Re-arm," *International Herald Tribune*, 21 Feb 2007, http://www.iht.com/articles/ap/2007/02/21/africa/ME-GEN-Israel-Hezbollah.php.

70. As explained in other chapters, the Israeli government initiated an investigation that became known as the Winograd Commission whilst the IDF established 70 study groups to analyze the lessons of The Second Lebanon War. Hezbollah was not entirely complacent as it later began a series of preparations for war in the spring of 2008. See Nicholas Blanford's "Hizbullah Militants Regroup Amid War Jitters," *Christian Science Monitor*, 14 April 2008."

71. Paul Wood, "Analysis: Operation Miscast Lead?" *BBC Online News*, 13 March 2009, http://news.bbc.co.uk/2/hi/middle_east/7940624.stm (accessed 19 March 2009).

72. Stephan Biddle and Jeffrey A. Friedman, *The 2006 Lebanon Campaign and the Future of Warfare: Implications For Army and Defense Policy* (Fort Leavenworth, Kansas: US Army Strategic Studies Institute, September 2008), xiv.

73. Ibid., xv.

74. "MI Chief: Hamas Hurt in Gaza, But Group Unlikely to Surrender," *Haaretz. com*, 11 Jan 2009, http://www.haaretz.com/hasen/spages/1054499.html.

75. "Tactics, Techniques and Procedures of the Islamic Resistance (IR), Hezbollah–Lebanon," *(UNCLASSIFIED/FOUO) TRADOC DCSINT Handbook No. 17*, (Fort Leavenworth, Kansas: March 2007), 22.

76. Ibid., 8. Quoted from Center for Strategic and International Studies (CSIS) source, http://www.csis.org/burke.

77. Makovsky and White, 48.

78. Biddle and Friedman, 45.

79. Biddle and Friedman, 45.

80. "Summer 2006 Lebanon War," 11.

81. Makovsky and White, 50.

82. "Summer 2006 Lebanon War," 22.

83. Biddle and Friedman, 35.

84. Biddle and Friedman, 39.

85. Spyer.

86. Makovsky and White, 48.

87. Spyer.

88. Makovsky and White, 48.

89. "Summer 2006 Lebanon War," 26.

90. "Hizbullah hits Israel's INS *Hanit* With Anti-ship Missile," *Jane's Defence Weekly*, 18 July 2006, http://www.janes.com/defence/news/jdw/jdw060718_1_ n.shtml.

91. Spyer.

92. Makovsky and White, 45.

93. Spyer.

94. Spyer.

95. Biddle and Friedman, 42.

96. Biddle and Friedman, 42

97. *TRADOC DCSINT Handbook No. 17*, 8.

98. Cordesman, "The 'Gaza War:' A Strategic Analysis," 15.

99. *TRISA Handbook No. 16*, 21.

100. Makovsky and White, p.48.

101. *TRADOC DCSINT Handbook No. 17*, 31.

102. "Summer 2006 Lebanon War," 29. Source was quoted in TRISA product. Original source Ron Scheifer, "Psychological Operations: a New Variation on an Age-old Art: Hezbollah versus Israel, *Studies in Conflict and Terrorism*, Volume 29 No. 1 (2006), http://www.informaworld.com/smpp/title~content=g725841507~db=all.

103. *TRISA Handbook No. 27*, 11.

104. Isabel Kershner, "Hamas to Start Paying Gaza Residents Compensation

and Reconstruction Aid," *New York Times*, 23 January 2009, http://www.nytimes.com/2009/01/23/world/middleeast/23mideast.html?fta=y.

105. Douglas Hamilton, "Gaza Group Revises Final Death Toll Figures," *Reuters*, 20 March 2009, www.reuters.com.

106. Roni Sofer, "Intelligence Sources Believe Hamas Damaged," *YNetnews.com*, 11 January 2009, http://www.ynet.co.il/english/articles/0,7340,L-3654264,00.html.

107. "Ending the War in Gaza," Middle East Briefing No.26.

108. Cordesman, "The 'Gaza War:' A Strategic Analysis," 9.

109. Quote from Interview with Abu Obeida, Izzedine al-Qassam Brigades spokesman, *Al-Hayat*, 17 December 2007, cited in *TRISA Handbook No. 27*, 20.

110. "Hamas's Military Buildup in the Gaza Strip," Intelligence and Terrorism Information Center, 7.

111. Omar Karmi, "Shoots of Recovery—Israeli Operation Leaves Hamas Weak But Alive," *Jane's Intelligence Review*, 12 Feb 2009, http://jir.janes.com/public/jir/index.shtml.

112. Jim Zanotti, "Israel and Hamas: Conflict in Gaza (2008-2009)," *Congressional Research Service*, 15 January 2009, 3, http://opencrs.com/document/R40101/2009-01-15.

113. Martin Kramer, comment on "Did Hamas Really Win in Gaza?" Harvard blog, Middle East Strategy at Harvard, comment posted on 28 January 2009, http://blogs.law.harvard.edu/mesh/2009/01/did-hamas-really-win-in-gaza/.

114. David Makovsky, "Preliminary Assessment of Israel's Operation Cast Lead," *PolicyWatch #1462*, 23 January 2009, The Washington Institute for Near East Policy, http://www.washingtoninstitute.org/templateC05.php?CID=2997.

115. Cordesman, "The 'Gaza War:' A Strategic Analysis," 42.

116. Cordesman, "The 'Gaza War:' A Strategic Analysis," 18.

117. Karmi, 12 Feb 2009.

118. Spyer.

119. Karmi.

120 Yaakov Katz, "Hamas Use of Children Was Monstrous," *Jerusalem Post*, 22 January 2009, http://www.jpost.com/servlet/Satellite?pagename=JPost%2FJPArticle%2FShowFull&cid=1232292939041.

121. Karmi.

122. Ethan Bronner, "Israel Lets Reporters See Devastated Gaza Site and Image of a Confident Military," *New York Times*, 16 Jan 2009, http://www.nytimes.com/2009/01/16/world/middleeast/16gaza.html.

123. David Bedein, "Israel Scores Initial Victories in Gaza War," *IsraelBehindTheNews.com*, 9 January 2009, http://israelvisit.co.il/cgi-bin/friendly.pl?url=Jan-09-09!firststage. Source cites a report from *The Middle East Newline*.

124. Anthony H. Cordesman, "The Fighting in Gaza: How Does It End?" *Center*

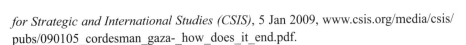
for Strategic and International Studies (CSIS), 5 Jan 2009, www.csis.org/media/csis/pubs/090105_cordesman_gaza-_how_does_it_end.pdf.

125. "Israel is Nearing Gaza Goals", *BBC News*, 11 January 2009, http://news.bbc.co.uk/2/hi/middle_east/7822786.stm.

126. Karmi.

127. Cordesman, "The 'Gaza War:' A Strategic Analysis," 58.

128. Cordesman, "The 'Gaza War:' A Strategic Analysis," 58.

129. "Hamas Probe to Unveil Military Failings Over Gaza," *AFP*, 26 January 2009, http://www.google.com/hostednews/afp/article/ALeqM5hL8Dwy9GU7nHS0Wga-S9Ty1jsGhJg.

130. Cordesman, "The 'Gaza War:' A Strategic Analysis," 59.

131. Cordesman, "The 'Gaza War:' A Strategic Analysis," 59.

132. Max Boot, "The Gaza Aftermath, Most Israelis Think They Won This Round," *Weekly Standard*, Volume 014, Issue 19, 2 February 2009, http://www.weeklystandard.com/Content/Public/Articles/000/000/016/052ggjlw.asp.

133. Martin Kramer, comment on "Did Hamas Really Win in Gaza?" Harvard blog, Middle East Strategy at Harvard, comment posted on 28 January 2009, http://blogs.law.harvard.edu/mesh/2009/01/did-hamas-really-win-in-gaza/.

134. Biddle and Friedman, xv.

Chapter 3

The Tactics of
Operation CAST LEAD

by
Lieutenant Colonel Abe F. Marrero
Command and General Staff School Center for Army Tactics

Scope

The purpose of this chapter is to review topics of interest at the tactical level of war in Operation CAST LEAD. The general military lessons learned from the Second Lebanon War will serve as a point of departure. In attempting a comparison of these two most recent military operations conducted by the Israeli Defense Force (IDF) it is important to note that Hamas is not Hezbollah and the terrain in Gaza (dense urban coastal desert) is quite different than the terrain in south Lebanon (hills, ridges, valleys and wadis). The common denominator then is the IDF and more specifically its performance in Operation CAST LEAD relative to its performance in the Second Lebanon War. The discussion will be limited to the tactical level of war although it is appreciated that the lines between strategic, operational, and tactical are often blurred and may in fact overlap.

Revisiting the Second Lebanon War

In keeping with the introspective trait of Israeli culture, the conduct and decision making by national and military leadership during the Second Lebanon War has been the subject of many inquiries and investigations (e.g., the Winograd Commission, headed by retired judge Eliyahu Winograd). At the operational level a review of the literature reveals a few generally agreed upon findings:[1]

- Airpower alone is not decisive.

- Precision fires without dominant maneuver are indecisive.

- Decisive operations are enhanced when precision airpower is coupled with combined arms ground maneuver.

The top military leader during the Second Lebanon War was Chief of the General Staff Lieutenant General Dan Halutz, the first Israeli Air Force (IAF) officer to hold the position. He was an ardent disciple of Effects Based Operations (EBO) believing that it would provide a less costly alternative to major ground operations.[2] In fact in 2002 he was quoted as stating that "Through the use of airpower supported by accurate intelligence, you can impose a siege, loiter over an area, maintain presence in an area, prevent movement or stop infiltration. All this can be accomplished from the air . . . and often more effectively and at less cost than artillery, tanks or ground forces."[3] A premise of EBO is that attacking the adversary's systems (e.g., command and control, communications, logistics) with precision-guided munitions vice combat formations would invoke an effect on his cognitive domain.[4] The theory that airpower alone could achieve strategic, operational, and tactical objectives was understandably attractive to a society that is self-described as casualty-averse.[5] To its credit, the IAF did manage to destroy most if not all of the Iranian supplied medium and long range missiles (*Zelzal* rocket launchers) within a few days of the commencement of hostilities.[6] But after approximately 15,000 combat sorties, Hezbollah *Katyusha* and *Qassam* rockets continued to rain on Israel, surging to over 200 on the last day of the war.[7] Clearly, the notion that airpower (using precision-guided munitions) alone could achieve national Israeli strategic objectives was misplaced.

At the tactical level, several issues stand out that shaped training in the years leading up to Operation CAST LEAD. In this short discourse, only two areas pertinent to Operation CAST LEAD will be explored, leadership and doctrine. Leadership in the IDF came under sharp criticism in the Winograd Commission (specifically Chapter 11, "Conclusions on IDF," Final Winograd Report, 30 January 2008) report. The years between Israel's unilateral withdrawal from Lebanon (2000) and the Second Lebanon War were characterized by security operations in Gaza and the West Bank. It was not uncommon in the years leading to the Second Lebanon War for commanders involved in security operations in Gaza and the West Bank to operate from static command posts in the rear.[8] It is important to note that the aforementioned security operations in Gaza and the West Bank were conducted predominately at the company and platoon level.[9] This practice became endemic and was in some cases manifested in the Second Lebanon War when commanders of Israeli forces entering combat in Lebanon were predisposed to be in rear command posts. As expressed by one senior IDF officer involved in leadership training, a kind of "COIN state of mind" set in with commanders and officers as a result of the continuous security operations in the occupied territories. In fact, prior to the Second Lebanon War training was focused on platoon level security operations.[10] This cognitive shift was further exacerbated by underfunding for readiness (command post exercises, combined arms training, brigade and battalion level maneuver exercises) in both the active ("mandatory" in Israeli parlance) and reserve forces. This became so pronounced that some battalion commanders' first live fire exercise during the Second Lebanon War was when they went into combat![11] These dynamics also imperceptibly impacted war fighting doctrine.

As a result of years involved in counterinsurgency operations, the IDF became quite adept at security patrols, cordon and search, and small unit raids at the expense of competency in larger unit (company and above) maneuvers, combat crew drills, live fire exercises, and combined arms operations. Well known for its expertise in maneuver warfare and combined arms operations, the IDF was not well prepared for operations at the scale, tempo, and terrain that they found themselves in July 2006 in south Lebanon. The lack of focus on combined arms training in high intensity combat (HIC) scenarios together with a precipitous cut in readiness funding conspired to set the conditions for less than favorable outcomes in Lebanon. These factors also had a deleterious impact on Israel's Reserve Forces.

In contrast to the US Armed Forces, the reserves are considered the core strength of the IDF.[12] The conscripted "mandatory" formations are expected to serve as a "trip wire" in case of attack and defend Israeli territory for as long as it takes to mobilize and deploy the reserves as its striking force. The "mandatory" formations undergo continual personnel turnover as draftees are released to the reserves and new inductees replace them; NCOs are mainly second-year conscripts with additional training. Reserve units are made up of experienced veterans who have served together for years and have higher discipline, élan and cohesion than their mandatory counterparts. Leading up to the Second Lebanon War reserve forces were lacking in training, equipment, and their mobilization call-up system was not exercised. Shockingly it was reported (by the State Comptroller) that there were entire reserve battalions that did not train in live-fire exercises for periods of four or five years.[13] In keeping with the "COIN mind set" the Reserves were also used extensively in security operations in Gaza and the West Bank and did not engage in major maneuver operations after the 2000 Intifada. Another issue mentioned in the Winograd Report was the ineffectual use of the Reserve Activation plan.[14] Despite contingency plans that existed in Northern Command for early mobilization of reserves in the event of ground operations requiring reinforcement, the Israeli political and military leadership failed to enact them. When the decision to activate the reserves was finally made on July 21, their late arrival was further hindered by unclear plans for their use and their integration into the ground campaign.[15]

The Intervening Years, 2006–2008

Israel, more so than other nations, exists in "an interwar period." Israel had less than two years in which to address the deficiencies and prepare for the inevitable next round of conflict. Halutz's replacement as Chief of Staff, army Lt. Gen. Gabi Ashkenazi, in September 2007 began improvements in both the material and intellectual condition of the Israeli Defense Forces. To address equipment problems he initiated a five-year military procurement plan that for the first time in more than a decade made significant investment in the land forces. The plan, Tefen 2012, included fielding hundreds of new *Merkava* Mark 4 tanks (and upgrades of the reserve's older model tanks to the Mark 4 standard), the development of a heavy armored personnel carrier (the *Merkava*-based *Namer* APC), and purchasing upgraded digital command and control systems and complimentary range of a unmanned ISR systems.[16]

The procurement priorities of the IDF's Tefen 2012 plan recognized the threats and limitations imposed by modern weapons coupled with asymmetric and hybrid warfare tactics. These methods were expected to be utilized by Israel's enemies' political movements and their various military arms in the near future. Materially, Ashkenazi, an experienced infantryman, set out to "strengthen the infantry brigades, enabling them to move and fight over any terrain facing high threat levels in [a] fire-saturated environment."[17] The lack of these types of vehicles had severely hindered the IDF's mobility in the Second Lebanon War in the face of ATGMs (anti-tank guided missiles) and mines and prevented the application of combined arms maneuver.

To compliment these material acquisitions, Ashkenazi shifted the IDF's emphasis back towards the traditional dominant role of land forces. He reversed the years of neglect and erosion in equipment modernization and training that had occurred after the withdrawal from Lebanon in 2000 and the subsequent focus on continuous low-intensity warfare in the occupied territories. This latter priority, as noted, was on small unit counter-insurgency tactics and equipment rather than offensive maneuver warfare. Commanders had come to rely on pin-point "perfect" intelligence from informants and continual surveillance in this environment rather than on the aggressive use of reconnaissance to fight for information. This neglect had resulted in a series of nasty surprises in the hillsides and towns of southern Lebanon in the summer of 2006 and Tefen 2012 set out to remedy the situation before the next conflict.

During this time the IDF made far-reaching changes to training that translated into doctrine and tactics that would address short comings exposed in the

Second Lebanon War. To better understand the doctrinal changes it might be useful to frame them in terms of the IDF Principles of War. Additionally, this will serve as another lens to view lessons learned from the Second Lebanon War. Almost all modern western armies have principles of war that form their leadership training and doctrine and the IDF is no exception. As defined in 1998, the IDF Principles of War are:[18]

1. Mission and Aim–Adherence to the mission by being guided by the aim.

2. Optimal utilization of forces.

3. Initiative and offensive.

4. Stratagem (loosely translated to surprise).

5. Concentration of efforts.

6. Continuity of action.

7. Depth and reserves.

8. Security.

9. Maintenance of morale and fighting spirit.

10. Simplicity.

In reference to the first principle (Mission and Aim) it was clear from the Winograd Commission report and other sources that this was violated.[19] At the strategic level, the objectives (ends) were selected that would be extremely difficult, if not impossible to achieve militarily (e.g., return of the two kidnapped IDF soldiers and disarmament of Hezbollah).[20] The indoctrination of EBO at the highest levels of the IDF further compounded the problem as mission orders to subordinate commands, couched in EBO and/or Systemic Operational Design (SOD) terms, were not clear and understandable (e.g. how do you translate *"cognitive perception of defeat"* into tactical terms?). It should come as no surprise that the IDF promptly returned to using a common lexicon throughout the force establishment in training and institutional organizations to reserve and active forces after what became known as The Second Lebanon War. The mandate was "train as you did before 2000."[21]

Optimal utilization of forces speaks to how different elements of the military are used separately or in combination to achieve objectives. The piecemeal fashion in which the IDF was employed in the Second Lebanon War is a testament to the outcomes if this principle is ignored. Accordingly, the IDF returned to tough and realistic combined arms training exercises. In addition, reserve forces underwent an increase in the frequency of readiness training. Towards this end, as part of Tefen 2012, the IDF established a program to methodically train reserve units and to conduct exercises that would establish habitual relations and integration with active units in specific theaters (e.g., Northern Command).[22]

The IDF's principles of initiative and the offensive spirit were lacking in 2006.[23] The "COIN mindset" with its attendant preoccupation with security operations, force protection, and commanders operating from static command posts (sometimes referred to as "plasma paralysis") have been discussed previously. To remedy these conditions the IDF training emphasized the traditional "lead from the front" ethos of the earlier, egalitarian Israeli nation in peril.[24] Additionally, training and exercises returned to decisive combined arms offensive operations.

The next three principles—stratagem, concentration of efforts, and continuity of actions—will be treated concurrently. Taken together, they represent the military conduct of the war. Even though it is widely accepted that Hezbollah was "surprised" at the overwhelming military response of Israel to the kidnapping of the two IDF soldiers, this surprise was not exploited.[25] The ground campaign was conducted in an almost reluctant fashion and forces launched uncoordinated battalion-sized raids piecemeal into Hezbollah-occupied southern Lebanon, mitigating the principle of concentration of effort. An example is the costly mission to take Bint Jbeil. Rather than adhering to the doctrinal principal of *offensive spirit* and bypassing this strong point for an armored drive to the Litani River (which, incidentally, is what the Northern Command prewar plans called for), the imperative communicated from Chief of the IDF General Staff Dan Halutz was to sieze Bint Jbeil because it symbolized Hezbollah success.[26] Rather than creating constant pressure on the enemy through audacious and decisive fire and maneuver, the principle of *continuity of actions*, the IDF instead became bogged down in a war of attrition in an enemy strongpoint. In the intervening years the IDF practiced war plans as they were written, emphasizing the elements of surprise, unity of effort, and fast-paced, high-tempo operations (continuity of actions) to knock the enemy from his plan and impose their will upon him.

In regard to depth and reserves two points warrant examination. First, concerning ground operations, the IDF leadership did not strive for operational reach (i.e. conducting ground operations to the Litani River) until much later in the campaign, choosing instead to conduct limited objective raids along the border. This played into the strength of Hezbollah's strategy by allowing it to employ an effective area defense, delaying the IDF through attrition, and permitting reinforcements and weapons systems to continue to stream south into the area while continuing to shell Israel with its rocket artillery. The IDF's piecemeal employment of combat forces along the entire front was symptomatic of the neglect of using a reserve to exploit success as was the aforementioned principle and tradition of the IDF. This was in sharp contrast to past campaigns in the 1967 Six Day War and 1973 Yom Kippur War which were characterized by large scale maneuver of ground forces and combined arms operations driving deeply into enemy territory in the early stages of fighting.[27]

The IDF compromised security by its reluctance to commit forces using combined arms doctrine (e.g., infantry and armor in mutual support). This has been attributed to the casualties inflicted on the opening day by successful Hezbollah anti-armor ambushes, which used "swarming" tactics—firing multiple rounds at a single tank. Subsequently, the ATGM became the weapon most feared by IDF troops.[28] This may have induced an excessive fear of casualties which translated to hesitant commanders and the focus of missions shifting to casualty retrieval/recovery.[29] In addition, morale and "fighting spirit" would be negatively impacted by the lack of cohesive and coherent missions and objectives.

To redress the noncompliance with their own principles of war, the IDF embarked on a return to the fundamentals that characterized their doctrine after 2006. To enhance battle command they conducted command post exercises at battalion, brigade and division level annually. There was a return to large-scale, combined and joint training. For example, the Northern Division (91st) conducted exercises to test readiness and incorporation of called-up reserve forces.[30] To hone full-spectrum operations in complex terrain, IDF soldiers trained in a mock Arab city built on a base in southern Israel. To add realism and to test asymmetric principles, role players were used for civilians, combatants and the media.[31] The IDF would soon have the opportunity to determine if the hard-earned lessons from the Second Lebanon War had been mastered.

Operation CAST LEAD—Implementing Lessons Learned

The shaping operation of the IDF's Operation CAST LEAD, though a major portion of the opening phase, was an air attack and its conduct is beyond the span of this treatise. Suffice it to say it was a carefully planned "decapitation" strike to kill selected Hamas leaders and destroy command facilities, weapons storage sites and smuggling tunnels. Large-scale ground operations commenced on 3 January and the air-land battle continued until 18 January 2009.[32] The major objectives for Operation CAST LEAD, as articulated by Israeli Defense Minister Ehud Barak, was to attack Hamas leadership and its infrastructure and "to force Hamas to stop its hostile activities against Israel."[33]

At the tactical level, this can be translated to the aforementioned targeting of key Hamas leaders, destroying Hamas' rocket firing capability, and destroying tunnels across the border used for smuggling arms, munitions, and personnel into Gaza. It appears that the campaign plan called for IDF ground forces to isolate (divide) north Gaza from south Gaza, taking control of Gaza's main north-south highway, the source of much of Hamas arms and sustainment.[34] From these maneuvers it is inferred that the end state involved isolating and securing Gaza City, destroying a significant amount of Hamas rocket and mortar squads, eliminating key Hamas military leadership (HVT), and destroying as many tunnels as can be located (especially along the Philadelphia corridor). How and to what extent this was accomplished will be the topic of the remainder of the paper. The war fighting functions (leadership, command and control, intelligence, movement and maneuver, fires, protection, sustainment, and information) will be used as a roadmap to examine IDF performance at the tactical level during Operation CAST LEAD. In addition, a descriptive snapshot of weapons employed during the most current operation will be included.

Leadership and C^2

Leadership at all levels showed a marked improvement as compared to performance during the Second Lebanon War. As was noted before, many commanders remained in fixed, robust command posts in 2006. In contrast, in Operation CAST LEAD commanders lead from the front and were in the midst of combat operations, resulting in injuries to several commanders. In the Second Lebanon War, the war was pretty much run from GHQ by the IDF Chief of Staff Lieutenant General Dan Halutz in Tel Aviv, slowing down the decision cycle. During CAST LEAD, the operations were orchestrated from Southern Command in coordination and consultation with GHQ.[35] Another significant change was at what level was battle command orchestrated from. In contrast to the Second Lebanon War being fought at the division level and its attendant command post-centric methods, Operation CAST LEAD was fought at the brigade level. Each brigade was given its own axis, objectives and mission and their progress was coordinated by the division HQ. This C^2 arrangement greatly improved the combat commander's responsiveness to the battle and afforded many more opportunities for initiative.

In a bold change to long-held Israeli modus operandi, brigade commanders were given control of key combat enablers—attack helicopters, unmanned aerial vehicles (UAVs), and an allotment of air sorties. In the past the control and apportionment of these assets were parochially retained by the IAF. This change was instrumental in enhancing tactical decision-making and providing brigade commanders superior agility and latitude in mission command.

The resulting orders and missions were clearly articulated using traditional and widely accepted doctrinal and tactical terms. Mission goals and objectives were unambiguous and measurable. The performance of commanders at all levels was evidence that the IDF had made significant changes in leadership, battle command, and C^2.

Intelligence

It's apparent from the targets successfully attacked by the IAF in the opening air phase of the operation that a comprehensive intelligence preparation of the battlefield (IPB) had been conducted. Several of Hamas' high value targets (HVTs) were successfully attacked including Azkariah al-Jamal, commander of Gaza City's rocket-launching squads, and Nizar Rayyan, the spiritual mentor of *Iz A-Din Al Qassam* Rocket Brigades.[36] It should also be noted that many of the HVTs that were targeted by the IDF managed to survive and elude Israeli forces, but were prevented from exercising effective C^2 by these continual survivability moves.

IDF soldiers were well-versed on Hamas weapons, tactics, and doctrine. UAVs (Hermes, Heron, and Searcher) were ubiquitous and provided continuous real-time thermal and visual intelligence to battalion and brigade command posts (CP). The UAVs flew 500 meters in front of advancing combat formations, transmitting color imagery of potential ambush sites and enemy dispositions. This capability promoted force protection, provided actionable target data and unparalleled situational awareness.[37] The IDF also formed robust intelligence "fusion" cells at the battalion and brigade level TOCs (tactical operation centers) manned with Arab-speaking combat interrogators (Arab linguists), geospatial specialists, and IAF liaisons. The IDF also benefited from intelligence provided by anti-Hamas entities (HUMINT) as well as SIGINT (signals intelligence) and COMINT (communications intelligence). The IDF's use of all-source intelligence collection and the technique of "pushing" products and collection assets down to the tactical level improved targeting and situational awareness.

Movement and Maneuver

After the air phase of the campaign, the land phase commenced during the early hours of 3 January with three brigade task forces supported by artillery attacking into Gaza proper. One brigade task force (Paratroopers Brigade) attacked from the north along the Mediterranean coast to drive Hamas forces out of their rocket-firing positions; a second brigade task force (Givati Brigade) penetrated south of Gaza City in the vicinity of the Karni crossing moving

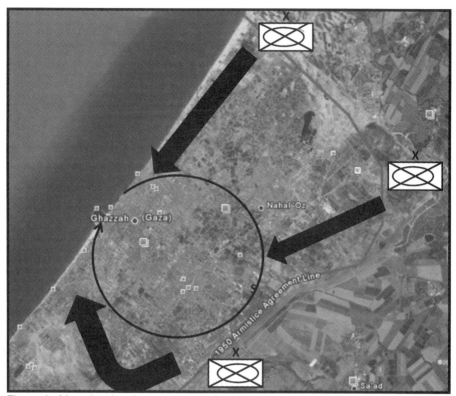

Figure 1. Map showing the movement of the three brigade task forces during the land phase of Operation CAST LEAD.

west to isolate Gaza City; and the third (Golani Brigade) in the center between the other two. This allowed the "Gaza Division" (162d Armored Division), with operational control of the brigade task forces, to isolate Gaza City and effectively cut it off from Gaza's main north-south highway.

Proceeded by UAVs, movement of combined arms formations avoided predictable avenues of approach and went in "heavy," using maneuver and firepower to preempt ambushes. To further pave the way there was extensive use of the *Tsefa* mine clearing system[38] to breach, clear, or explosively reduce minefields (its intended use) and to blast movement corridors through built-up areas.[39] Most operations were conducted during the cover of darkness to take advantage of the lack of Hamas night vision devices and maximize the IDF's training in night operations. The IDF brigades used maneuver to cause the enemy to react, move from prepared positions, and expose themselves to fires or assault. Upon approaching objectives or built -up areas, infantry dismounted to make the attack supported by armor and engineers, counter to previous conflicts (e.g., Six Day War, Yom Kippur War) in which armor was the "tip of

Figure 2. IDF D-9 Bulldozer during Operation CAST LEAD.

the spear" supported by infantry. In fact a new "tank" appeared—the heavily armored Caterpillar D-9 bulldozer which was used to create new avenues of approach that bypassed likely ambush sites, mine fields, IEDs, and pre-chambered demolitions (the feared "belly mines" that destroyed two IDF tanks in the Second Lebanon War).

Maneuver was accompanied by heavy doses of fires to suppress enemy ambushes and to preserve the offensive spirit. All of these operations were executed at a high tempo to sustain the initiative and prevent Hamas from regrouping and consolidating a viable defense. Dismounted IDF infantry avoided obvious zones of fire such as intersections and open areas. For the most part IDF units maneuvered to bypass Hamas strong points.[40] If it was necessary to secure them, the preferred method was through the judicious use of fires and D-9 bulldozers. In sharp contrast to the 2006 campaign, the Israeli ground forces returned to the basic fundamentals that had served it so well in the past—audacious combined arms maneuver warfare supported by devastating firepower.

Fires

In Operation CAST LEAD the Gaza Division deployed with at least one fires brigade. Each brigade had IAF liaison officers in the CP and was provided with a slice of attack helicopter, fixed-wing aviation, and UAVs. As alluded to before, having up to twelve UAVs constantly flying over the Gaza strip provided numerous targets for these assets. Targeting data was also provided by SIGINT and HUMINT along with the UAV imagery. Regarding electronic warfare, it appears that the IDF dominated the electromagnetic spectrum as they were able to jam most of Hamas' TV, radio and cellular communications.[41] This was not the case during the Second Lebanon War where Hezbollah proved to be quite adept in the use, exploitation and protection of the electromagnetic spectrum.

There has been a great deal of negative press coverage on the alleged use by the IDF of incendiary white phosphorous (WP) rounds. It should be noted that the Law of Land Warfare does not prohibit the use of WP against enemy personnel.[42] Typically WP is used to create "immediate smoke" since other types of smoke rounds cannot provide an instantaneous smokescreen. The IDF used the US-made M825A1 smoke round that detonates in the air and showers the ground with small felt wedges soaked in WP.[43] These are far less lethal than the traditional ground-bursting WP rounds used by combatants in past conflicts.[44] It is not uncommon for leaders to use WP smoke in combat to obscure enemy observation, screen to provide concealment for friendly troops in contact, their movement, or casualty evacuation or to mark a position. It is not inconceivable that the IDF's use of WP smoke rounds in urban areas may have inadvertently caused casualties. The IDF and various human rights agencies are investigating the cases where WP was used in urban areas.[45]

Protection

After being bloodied in the previous campaign in south Lebanon, the casualty-averse IDF instituted stringent force protection measures to further minimize losses. In addition to casualties due to combat, the greatest threat to IDF soldiers was the danger of abduction by Hamas. A reported Hamas tactic was to lure IDF soldiers into buildings or tunnels with the intent of kidnapping them.[46] Accordingly, IDF units established and practiced anti-abduction tactics, techniques, and procedures (TTPs). Of interest is the fact that all infantry units were accompanied by K-9 units—*Oketz* ("Sting") detachments.[47] With origins in *Haganah* circa 1939, these *Sayeret*-affiliated units consist of a handler and his/her dog (Belgian Shepherd or Malinois being the preferred breed) trained in a specialty, e.g., attack, tracking, explosives detection, weapons and munitions detection, and search and rescue. In a particularly salient force protection TTP, *Oketz* teams would enter a structure first to allow the dogs to search for explosives, booby traps, and hidden combatants.[48] This tactic was undoubtedly instrumental in reducing IDF human casualties as several dogs were killed and wounded and their use proved an effective deterrent to abduction attempts.[49]

The IDF entry into buildings was effected by breaching (blowing or knocking holes through walls) thereby avoiding potentially booby-trapped doors and windows.[50] Booby traps, IEDs, and ambush sites were further mitigated by the liberal use of heavily-armored D-9 bulldozers to create corridors through buildings and walls. This had the added benefit of negating Hamas's planned fields of fire and the required line of sight for successful employment of RPGs and ATGMs. Considering the scope of the operation, its tempo, the complex urban environment, and the inherent advantage of well dug-in defenders, the relatively small number of IDF or collateral civilian casualties is remarkable. This is attributable to the lessons from the Second Lebanon War being well-heeded by the IDF and subsequent development and enforcement of effective force protection measures.

Photo courtesy of the Israeli Defense Force

Figure 3. An IDF Oketz K-9 team.

Sustainment

One of the findings cited in the Winograd Commission Report was the lack of adequate equipment and supplies experienced by units involved in the Second Lebanon War. To remedy the problem the IDF instituted a more effective logistics organization and sustainment procedures. In Operation CAST LEAD brigade support areas pushed supplies to battalion forward support areas, which then distributed the supplies and ammunition down to companies. Priority of combat service support was also revamped: Unlike the Second Lebanon War, casualty evacuation/recovery did not become the main effort and bring units to a halt. Instead, emphasis was placed upon maintaining forward momentum and multiple modes of casualty evacuation (CASEVAC) down to the company-level were instituted using light ground, armored and helicopter ambulances.

Information

Information operations (IO) will receive comprehensive coverage in a separate chapter, however a few points warrant mention in this section. The IDF took extreme, but not unprecedented, measures to augment operational security (OPSEC) and exert some modicum of control over the media. Firstly, the IDF confiscated the cell phones of soldiers involved in the operation. Second, the international media was barred from entering the Gaza Strip once hostili-

Photo courtesy of the Israeli Defense Force

Figure 4. Example of a D-9 bulldozer created corridor through a building wall.

ties commenced with the exception of a small group which were accompanied by the IDF. As mentioned in the Fires paragraph, the IDF was successful in jamming of all electronic modes of Hamas' communication. Of interest is the psychological impact this IO line of effort had on the target. It was reported that Palestinians "believe(ed) we could triangulate on terrorists' cell phones to find them, even when the phone was turned off."[51] Combined with the need to continually move to prevent being struck by precision fires, this denial of the electronic spectrum greatly hindered Hamas' C^2. How the IDF engaged the IO line of effort is a study in and of its self and will provide more valuable findings relevant to the Long War.

Weapons Systems Employed—A Snapshot.

Operation CAST LEAD featured a few new or improved IDF weapon systems. Listed below is a short nontechnical description.

• Robotics. During CAST LEAD there was extensive use of robots to enter buildings and tunnels. One of the robots used by forces was the *Bull Island*, which is a gimbal-mounted camera inside a clear plastic sphere about the size of a tennis ball. This can be thrown into any building, room or stairwell prior to soldiers entering. The camera transmits 360-degree imagery to a terminal with the troops waiting on the outside of the structure (or around a street corner).

• Anti-structure munitions. The Matador missile was originally developed by Israel's Rafael Armament Development Authority as an evolved version of the German Armburst shoulder fired anti-tank missile used as a Shoulder Launched Breaching Munition. Another anti-tank guided weapon that was modified as an anti-structural munition for operations in Gaza was first employed during the Second Lebanon War, the PB500A1 laser-guided "bunker-buster" bomb. Based on the US Mk-83 (1,000-lb) "dumb" bomb it is fitted with a penetrator warhead and laser guidance kit. It is reportedly capable of penetrating up to 7-ft (2 m) of reinforced concrete.[52]

Conclusion

At 0200 on 18 January, 2009, Israel declared that it would unilaterally observe a cease fire ending 22 days of intense combat in the Gaza Strip. There is an inherent risk in attempting an analysis of an operation before the smoke has cleared. No doubt more complete and reliable information will become available in the weeks and months to come. However, there is value in capturing the immediate and unfiltered thoughts of the conflict through the lens of first impressions. Against this backdrop the following conclusions are submitted.

The question that was posed was, to what extent did the IDF implement the lessons learned in the Second Lebanon War in Operation CAST LEAD? An examination of IDF actions using the Warfighting Functions articulated in US Army Field Manual 3-0 *Operations* as a framework suggests that its ground forces did indeed demonstrate evidence of having internalized and implemented the hard-earned lessons. At the campaign level the notion that airpower is decisive without a cohesive and decisive ground campaign was rejected. In Operation CAST LEAD the air phase was the shaping operation and the air-land phase the decisive operation. Rather than trying to manage the war from Central Command in Tel Aviv, the IDF orchestrated the battle from its Southern Command HQ. This shortened chain of command reduced confusion and friction as well as increased reaction time for engaged forces to implement orders.

At the tactical level, IDF leadership and C^2 were clearly addressed in the intervening years. Commanders once again were leading from the front and providing understandable mission orders with lucid objectives and intent. The war was fought at the brigade level and brigade commanders were equipped with the combat enablers necessary to allow for tactical agility and success. These provisions greatly reduced the decision cycle and response time for commanders to influence their battle through fires and maneuver.

Movement and maneuver also showed a sharp contrast between the 2006 war in Lebanon and the campaign in Gaza. Combat operations were, as noted, brigade-centric with overall command executed by the Gaza Division. The three brigades involved in the initial thrust into Gaza were task-organized down to the battalion level with necessary enablers (e.g., special engineer units, interrogators, dog handlers) attached rather than centralized. High-tempo combined arms maneuver with overpowering firepower were conducted at night to great advantage for the attacking IDF forces. Movement and maneuver avoided existing avenues of approach and used D-9 bulldozers and explosives to craft "corridors." The IDF went in heavy using fires to suppress and neutralize the enemy.

Fires were more responsive due to a change in organization and doctrine. IAF liaison officers were posted to each brigade TOC. Brigade commanders were allocated attack helicopters, UAVs, and CAS (close air support) sorties that were previously under the control of the IAF in Tel Aviv. The IDF also used electronic attack effectively to shape the battlefield.

The number of IDF casualties was remarkably small despite fighting in complex terrain against an enemy that was operating from prepared defensive positions on internal lines. Clearly the force protection measures taken by the IDF was exceptionally effective with no kidnapped or unrecovered soldiers and only a few casualties were a result of friendly fire (all apparently due to a malfunctioning artillery round). Noteworthy, too, was the ubiquitous use of robots and canines to "clear" buildings and other urban structures. Using D-9 armored bulldozers to create alternative routes of ingress and anti-structure munitions to blow holes in walls lowered the exposure of soldiers to booby traps, IEDs, mines, and ambushes while gaining a foothold.

There will be well-informed pundits that will expose mistakes and leverage criticism on the performance of the IDF (and Hamas) during Operation CAST LEAD. As more comprehensive analysis is compiled additional information will surface that may challenge the findings articulated here. But this early exposé suggests that there was vast improvement in the conduct of operations in CAST LEAD. Whatever lessons emerge from this latest chapter will no doubt be put to the test in the next round of conflict in the Middle East.

NOTES

1. John Antal (US Army, Ret), "Flashpoint Gaza Analysis" *Armchairgeneral. com,* 4 January, 2009, under "Flashpoint Gaza: the Israeli Defense Forces (IDF) Launches 'Operation CAST LEAD,'" http://www.armchairgeneral.com/wordpress/wp-content/uploads/gaza-flashpoint-update-0109.pdf (accessed 7 January 2009), 4.

2. Sarah E. Kreps, "The 2006 Lebanon War: Lessons Learned," *Parameters,* Vol. XXXVII, No. 1, Spring 2007: 78.

3. Dan Halutz, "IDF Shake-Up Over Hezbollah War: Unconventional War Revealed Failures of Leadership and Strategy," *Defense News* (2007), quoted in JINSA Online (March 2007), http://www.jinsa.org/articles/articles.html/function/view/categoryid/154/documentid/3736/history/3,2360,6 54,154,3736.

4. Matt M. Matthews, *We Were Caught Unprepared: The 2006 Hezbollah-Israeli War. The Long War Series Occasional Paper 26* (Fort Leavenworth, KS: Combat Studies Institute Press, 2008).

5. Russell W. Glenn, *All Glory is Fleeting: Insights from the Second Lebanon War,* Santa Monica, CA: RAND, 2008), p. 19. This document is not available to the general public at the present time.

6. Anthony H. Cordesman, "The Lessons of the Israel-Hezbollah War: A Briefing," (briefing, slide 27, Center for Strategic and International Studies, March 12, 2008).

7. Ibid., slide 25.

8. "The Second Lebanon War: Three Perspectives," (Joint Center for Operational Analysis paper, US Joint Forces Command, 1 May 2008), 8.

9. Col. Ronen Shviki (IDF), interview by author, 23 February 2009.

10. Ibid.

11. Ibid.

12. Christopher Jenkins, "Back to Basics: Deterrence and the IDF," Foreign Policy Centre Fresh Insight Paper, http://fpc.org.uk/fsblob/1027.pdf, (accessed 24 February 2009), 5.

13. Ibid.

14. Ibid., "The Second Lebanon War: Three Perspectives," 8.

15. Matt M. Matthews, *Occasional Paper 26—We Were Caught Unprepared: The 2006 Hezbollah-Israeli War* (Fort Leavenworth, KS: Combat Studies Institute Press) 44.

16. David Eshel, "Israel sets the Stage for a Massive, $60 Billion Military Build-up," *Defense Update,* September 3, 2007, http://defense-update.com/analysis/analysis_030907_israel.htm (accessed 27 February 2009).

17. Ibid; see also Eshel's article "Israel Launches Namer armored Infantry Fighting Vehicle Program" in *Defense Update* for the IDF's incorporation of the lessons learned in the Second Lebanon War as applied to combat developments. Israel, ironically, pioneered the use of heavy APCs in its conversion of surplus Centurion or captured T-55 main battle tanks into infantry fighting vehicles or combat engineer vehicles. The Namer program includes an armored ambulance to evacuate casualties from the direct fire zone. The Merkava and Namer variants are equipped with advanced

composite armor, reactive armor, and the Trophy Active Protection system (APS), the latter being retrofitted on to IDF M113 and Stryker variants, as well.

18. *IDF Dictionary of Terms* (Ministry of Defense, 1998), 484.

19. Cordesman, slide 39.

20. Jenkins, 2.

21. Shiviki interview.

22. Jenkins, 6.

23. "The Second Lebanon War: Three Perspectives," 7.

24. Author notes from briefing by Eliot Cohen to USA CGSOC, 17 Sept. 2006.

25. Yaakov Amidror, Major General (IDF), "Winning Counterinsurgency War: The Israeli Experience," *Strategic Perspectives*, 33, http://www.jcpa.org/text/Amidror-perspectives-2.pdf

26. Ibid., 32.

27. Jenkins, 5.

28. Shiviki interview.

29. See CALL IRR where higher HQs interfered and prohibited/mandated "tank ambulance" to go forward, etc.

30. Anthony H. Cordesman, "The 'Gaza War:' A Strategic Analysis," (Washington DC: Center for Strategic and International Studies, February 2009): 37, http://www.csis.org/media/csis/pubs/090202_gaza_war.pdf.

31. Gwen Ackerman, "Israel Applying Lessons From Lebanon to Gaza Fighting (Update 1)," *Bloomberg.com*, 6 January 2009, http://www.bloomberg.com/apps/news?pid=20601109&sid=ajkGMjpN05.k&refer=exclusive (accessed 20 February 2009).

32. Cordesman, "The 'Gaza War,'" 40.

33. Cordesman, "The 'Gaza War,'" 37.

34. Antal, "Flashpoint Gaza Analysis," 5.

35. Cordesman, "The 'Gaza War,'" 39.

36. Amidror, "Winning Counterinsurgency War," 5.

37. Haamimhagolan [pseud.], comment on "Air-to-Ground Weapons Selection During Operation Cast Lead," Israel Military Forum, comment posted 25 January 2009, http://www.israelmilitary.net/showthread.php?t=8875&highlight=Air-to-Ground+Weapons+Selection+Operation+Cast+Lead (accessed 24 February 2009).

38. The Tsefa ("Viper") mine clearing system is a rocket-launched chain of small charges designed to clear lanes. Photos available at http://www.defense-update.com/news/6702carpet.htm.

39. Cordesman, "The 'Gaza War,'" 40.

40. Anthony H. Cordesman, "The Fighting in Gaza: How Does It End? (And, Will It End?)" (Washington DC: Center for Strategic and International Studies, 5 January 2009): 2, http://www.csis.org/media/csis/pubs/090105_cordesman_gaza-_how_does_it_end.pdf.

41. Joel J. Sprayregen, "The Inside Story of Operation Cast Lead," *American Thinker*, 27 January 2009, http://www.americanthinker.com/2009/01/inside_story_of_israels_succes.html (accessed 24 February 2009).

42. Field Manual No. 27-10, *The Law of Land Warfare* dated 18 July 1956 with Change 1 dated 15 July 1976, Chapter 2, Section II, paragraph 36 (Washington DC:

Department of the Army), 25. It reads:

36. Weapons Employing Fire. The use of weapons which employ fire, such as tracer ammunition, flamethrowers, napalm and other incendiary agents, against targets requiring their use is not violative of international law. They should not, however, be employed in such a way as to cause unnecessary suffering to individuals.

43. The 155-mm M825A1 smoke WP is a separate-loading base-ejection smoke-producing projectile. It uses a sealed canister containing 116 felt wedges saturated in WP that spontaneously ignite upon release and fall to the ground producing smoke. The felt wedges can cause burns if they strike or land upon personnel, though they are about the size and weight of a door stop, can easily be flicked away (author's experience).

44. Older types of shells exploded on impact and released their white phosphorus in a burst for screening, spotting and signaling purposes though they have an additional incendiary effect on a target and possess casualty-producing effects (e.g. "White Phosphorus Shell (M110 Series); WP is used for marking, screening, obscuring, and incendiary effects. It is effective against vehicles, POL storage areas, etc." Marine Corps Warfighting Publication (MCWP) 3-16.1, *Artillery Operations* (Washington, DC: Department Of The Navy Headquarters United States Marine Corps, 2002).

45. Michael Evans and Sheera Frenkel, "Gaza Victims' Burns Increase Concern Over Phosphorus," *The Times*, January 8, 2009, http://www.timesonline.co.uk/tol/news/world/middle_east/article5470047.ece?sub=wp.

46. *Israeli Defense Forces Newsletter*: 3, http://berlin.mfa.gov.il/mfm/Data/153624.pdf (accessed 24 February 2009).

47. Yaakov Katz, "Barak: Hamas Was Dealt a Blow It Never Imagined," *Jerusalem Post*, 21 January, 2009, http://www.jpost.com/servlet/Satellite?pagename=JPost/JPArticle/ShowFull&cid=1232292928942, (accessed 3 March 2009). Oketz dog-handlers are often task-organized to other units in the case of a particular need for their specialized skills. Though not affiliated with the IDF Paratroopers Brigade, Oketz handlers wear the same distinctive red berets and the unit's graduation ceremony is held at the Paratroopers headquarters.

48. Amira Hass, "Palestinians: IDF First Sends Dogs Into Gaza Homes, Then Soldiers," *haaretz.com*, 11 January 2009, http://www.haaretz.com/hasen/spages/1054133.html (accessed 24 February 2009).

49. There is some controversy within Israel over the use of these dogs as the Nazis used the same breeds in concentration camps to guard and intimidate the inmates. Israeli society is rife with these cultural sensitivities.

50. Sprayregen, 1

51. Sprayregen, 1

52. "Air-to-Ground Weapons Selection During Operation Cast Lead."

Chapter 4

Information Strategies Against A Hybrid Threat:

What the Recent Experience of Israel Versus Hezbollah/Hamas Tell The US Army

by
Lieutenant Colonel Michael D. Snyder
TRADOC Intelligence Support Activity and Capabilities
Development Integration Division–Informaiton Operations

Introduction

From the 2006 Lebanon War (Operation CHANGE OF DIRECTION) to the 2008-2009 Gaza Operation (Operation CAST LEAD) the Israelis were confronted with what is characterized as a Hybrid Threat. The following is the initial step in a comparative study of how information strategies were used in both cases. The hybrid adversary, as opposed to a conventional force, will almost always survive to fight another day. Determining who won and who lost will therefore often be a matter of perception. The United States Army and the Israeli Defense Forces (IDF) both have a strong interest in managing the perceptions of key target audiences. Doing so can make the difference with respect to gaining and maintaining an operational advantage.

The Rising Importance of the Information Battle

Hybrid War

While in some parts of the world the United States must still contend with near-peer competitors, in the greater Middle East major state-to-state conflict is not the likely model of warfare that we will encounter. In the future landscape of conflict the US Army is more likely to face what Frank Hoffman has aptly described as "Hybrid Threats." According to Hoffman, "Hybrid Wars incorporate a range of different modes of warfare, including conventional capabilities, irregular tactics and formations, terrorist acts including indiscriminate violence and coercion and criminal disorder."[1] In warfare against a Hybrid Threat there are no sequential phases of combat. The military can find itself engaged simultaneously in peacekeeping, major combat operations, and reconstruction and development. The US Army is currently contending with hybrid threats in Iraq, Afghanistan, and elsewhere. This experience has led to the adoption of an operational philosophy of persistent conflict.

In Hybrid Warfare, as in all types of warfare, information activities take on a particular importance. Adversaries who employ this method of warfare seek to draw conventional forces into combat in populated areas where the loyalty of the population can become the center of gravity in the conflict. In post-modern warfare the simple red-force versus blue-force dynamic does not apply. Between the red and the blue are other groups whose attitudes and perceptions of the conflict directly affect the power balance. To achieve lasting results from military intervention, it is therefore necessary to influence the civilian population's attitude toward our goals and how they perceive our actions to accomplish the goals.

Integral to accomplishing this task is a coordinated full-spectrum information effort that integrates all capabilities including information engagement[2] and activities in cyberspace (e.g. new media, web based communities, etc). Moreover, full-spectrum information activities must be fully integrated with combat operations.

The battle over perceptions is more than simply important; it is actually the heart of the matter. "It's now fundamentally an information fight," David Kilcullen says. The enemy gets that, and we don't yet." When they attack Humvees, for instance, "they're not doing that because they want to reduce the number of Humvees we have in Iraq by one. They're doing it because they want spectacular media footage of a burning Humvee."[3] For the adversaries, managing the perception of key target audiences is the single most important aspect of planning an operation. Psychological effects are the desired endstate of combat operations. The importance to the information fight is evidenced by the fact that al-Qaeda, Hezbollah, and Hamas all have highly sophisticated propaganda organizations. Hezbollah and Hamas operate television stations which broadcast a wide range of programming including children's shows. Both organizations reach audiences well beyond their immediate spheres of political control. Their close political ties to Iran ensure that their key themes and messages will also enjoy the full support of the Iranian state propaganda apparatus. Current communications trends suggest that this model will only spread through the region.

It is reasonable to assume that a hybrid adversary who operates amongst a civilian population will very likely, at least at first, understand the human terrain better than US forces. In the communications battle, therefore, the adversary will begin from a point of advantage. Before the United States places boots on the ground the adversary will know his local target audiences and will likely have sophisticated communications machinery in place to reach them. This may be called "cultural competency." Cultural competence does not equate to organic understanding as this takes long-term immersion. Cultural competence comprises four components:

• Awareness of one's own cultural worldview

• Attitude towards cultural differences

• Knowledge of different cultural practices and worldviews

• Cross-cultural skills. Developing cultural competence results in an ability to understand, communicate with, and effectively interact with people across cultures

There is a lesson to be learned here: Combat operations must be reconciled with a comprehensive influence strategy to meet the hybrid threat. If a kill-or-capture operation eliminates a military target but in the process alienates the surrounding civilian population (or otherwise undermines political legitimacy) then the military operation, however technically successful, must be judged as an overall failure.[4]

The Israeli Experience of Hybrid War

Recent Israeli experience is particularly helpful as a guide to understanding the complexities of the information battle in Hybrid War. In the last three years Israel has engaged in two major military operations against adversaries employing hybrid operational approaches: the Second Lebanon War against Hezbollah in July-August 2006 and Operation CAST LEAD against Hamas in Gaza in December 2008-January 2009. The importance of the information battle and how they were both handled differently was particularly apparent to the Israelis who drew a number of important lessons from their Lebanon experience and then applied them to the Gaza conflict. There is much to be gained from an analysis of the Israeli process of adaptation. The Israeli experience sheds light both on the general problem of Hybrid War information activities and on specific tactics for dealing with it.

A word of caution is warranted. Though similar, the Israeli and United States experiences are by no means identical. Israel and the United States have vast differences in terms of legal and organizational structures, international and domestic political contexts and historical experience. Consequently, some of the tactics that Israel has employed are not appropriate in the American context. This paper, therefore, is an effort to extract lessons of a general nature from the specifics of the Israeli experience.

The Adversary's Strategy

The Civilian-Victim Narrative

One aspect of the strategy is the civilian-victim theme. With respect to the information strategies of their respective adversaries, the United States and Israel face challenges that are very similar, if not identical. For nearly two decades, the wartime propaganda of the Middle Eastern opponents of both countries has been remarkably similar and consistent. Whether we are speaking of Saddam Hussein in the 1990s, or al-Qaeda in Iraq, the Taliban, Hamas, or Hezbollah, the core message has been the same: "You (Israelis or Americans, fill in the blank) are killing innocent women and children or supporting someone who is." The state media of Iran and Syria have frequently amplified this message, which, on close inspection is actually the centerpiece of a full-blown information strategy. Even though this same theme can be used against Hezbollah, Hamas or al-Qaeda, it does not surface unless there is a ground swell from the population and the atrocities so great that it cannot be ignored.

As an example, on one level, the theme of civilian victims is part of a larger narrative that depicts the United States and its allies as the implacable opponents of Muslims. In many Muslim countries a significant percentage of people who emphatically reject the beliefs and tactics of terrorist groups nevertheless are receptive to the claim that the United States military (to say nothing of the Israelis) is conducting a global war against Islam and Muslims. The civilian-victim message, therefore, cleverly exploits identity politics to tap into an ingrained distrust of American and Israeli motives.

But identity politics is only one factor at work—and not the most important one. This propaganda also has a universal appeal. It cuts across ethnic and religious lines, striking a powerful resounding chord wherever people harbor doubts, for whatever reason, regarding the efficacy of military force in the fight against terrorist organizations. It draws strength from the natural sympathy that people everywhere feel when they witness the suffering that war entails. It is in the interest of groups such as Hamas, Hezbollah, and al-Qaeda to emphasize this theme precisely because their actual ideologies do not resonate widely beyond the ranks of the ideologically indoctrinated.

The American and Israeli militaries are formidable and therefore easily portrayed as heavy-handed and indiscriminate in their use of force, consequently they are often characterized as Goliaths. The next point is that many in the world are predisposed to see any group that is opposed to the US or Israeli army as a David. In an age of instantaneous global communications the civilian-victim theme turns this predisposition into a powerful asymmetric tool of Hybrid Warfare. The theme, when successfully deployed, places powerful political constraints on the use of conventional forces. In the case of the IDF, two Israeli researchers describe the dilemma as follows: "In order to deter, the IDF has to appear and operate like a Goliath. Yet, everytime it appears and operates like a Goliath, it instantly loses media points."

This strategic dilemma hit the Israelis particularly hard during the Second Lebanon War, which unfolded against a background of tension between the international media and the IDF. Before examining the lessons learned from Lebanon, it is useful to bear in mind three separate episodes in the history of IDF-media relations. Taken together, these define a basic strategic problem for the IDF, which we might conveniently refer to as "the Civilian-Victim Dilemma": the loss of legitimacy that democratic armies suffer as a result of reports (real, exaggerated, or faked) that create the impression that military action is causing great harm to innocent civilians. It is a challenge that the United States military fully shares with the IDF. In a Hybrid War it has the potential to sap the legitimacy of United States actions among important allies, increase the power of a hybrid adversary, and undermine the support for the war effort at home.

The Jenin "Massacre": Media Exaggeration

Between 3 and 11 April 2002, at the height of the Second Intifada, a pitched battle broke out between the IDF and Palestinian militants in the West Bank city of Jenin. The coverage of this episode by the international press has led some Israelis to conclude that the European press is implacably biased against the IDF.

On March 29, Ariel Sharon launched Operation DEFENSIVE SHIELD and ordered the IDF to reoccupy parts of the West Bank that had been evacuated as part of the Oslo Accords. According to the UN report on the subject, after the Israeli forces withdrew on April 18, "at least fifty-two Palestinians, of whom up to half may have been civilians, and twenty-three Israeli soldiers were dead."[5] The near equality between the number of Israeli and Palestinian combatants killed suggests that the IDF engaged in house-to-house fighting and, in an effort to avoid civilian casualties, refrained from deploying indiscriminate use of air power. Be that as it may, during the fighting itself the European press published widespread Palestinian accusations of a massacre complete with descriptions of the stench of death and claims that whole families had been crushed beneath the rubble. Questionable Palestinian sources were quoted uncritically. In addition, many voices in the press expressed indignation, raised the call for war crimes investigations, and demanded an immediate cessation of violence. Representative of the exaggerations was the *Times* of London, which, though usually considered a paragon of journalistic responsibility, carried an article in which its correspondent stated that "rarely in more than a decade of war reporting from Bosnia, Chechnya, Sierra Leone, Kosovo, have I seen such deliberate destruction, such disrespect for human life."[6]

That a respected paper would compare a battle that killed twenty-six civilians to conflicts that indiscriminately killed many thousands left a residue of mistrust in some Israeli circles. Beyond the bad feelings that the episode engendered, there also stood a significant challenge to the effectiveness of military operations. First, plausible claims of mass civilian casualties generate immediate international sympathy particularly in the Arab world and Europe and increasingly in the United States, too. This sympathy translates into intense diplomatic pressure on the Israelis to halt operations (while the United States military sometimes faces such harsh press scrutiny, as it did in it Fallujah, does not usually translate this into immediate and powerful political pressure to halt operations).

When confronted with accusations of disproportionate force causing widespread civilian deaths, claims of war crimes, etc., Israeli spokesman find themselves on the horns of a dilemma. Firstly, they are not in a position to deny the claims, because, more often than not, they do not have at their disposal full information about what has happened on the ground. In the heat of battle even those directly involved in the fighting do not necessarily know the impact of their actions on the opposing side. On the other hand, failing to respond at all to the accusations risks appearing callus or indifferent to civilian suffering and thereby increasing international outrage. Caught between these two options, Israeli spokesmen have occasionally faltered, as did the IDF spokesman Ron Kitri. On 12 April, Kitri increased international indignation by mistakenly admitting that there were "apparently hundreds" killed. He later retracted this statement.[7]

Muhammad al-Durrah: Media Fabrication

Because the publicity surrounding civilian casualties is in fact a valuable tool for weakening Israel politically, there is a conscious effort by some Israeli adversaries to manufacture images of suffering and death. The most famous of these is the supposed killing by Israeli soldiers of Muhammad al-Durrah, a young boy who appeared to have died on September 30, 2000 at Netzarim junction in Gaza. Video images of al-Durrah's death were captured during an exchange of fire between Palestinian demonstrators and IDF soldiers who were hunkered down in a guard post overlooking the crossroads. The heart-rending images of the boy's final moments, as he crouched next to his father to avoid the gunfire, were captured by a Palestinian, Talal Abu Rahma, and a free-lance cameraman working for France 2 Television. Abu Rahma later delivered the footage to Charles Enderlin of France 2 who, though not present during the event, reported on French television that al-Durrah was killed by Israeli fire. The footage quickly spread throughout the world, evoking deep sympathies and damaging the reputation of the IDF. President Clinton himself expressed regret and dismay at al-Durrah's death. In the Arab world, al-Durrah immediately became an iconic figure representing the cruelty of Israel toward the Palestinian people. Songs were composed in his honor, streets and parks named after him, postage stamps imprinted with his image.

Not long after the event, however, doubts began to emerge regarding its accuracy. Today credible independent observers have concluded, based on analysis of extensive film footage and bullet angles, that the Israeli soldiers were probably not responsible for the death of al-Durrah. Vexed questions remain. Did the boy actually die, or was the entire episode fabricated? If he did die, who killed him? A significant school of thought, headed by Professor Richard Landes at Boston University, argues that the most likely explanation is that the event was entirely staged.[8] Landes has coined the term "Pallywood" (Palestinian+Hollywood) to refer to the use of staged productions of civilian casualties conducted before complicit camera crews who pass the clips to Western and Arab media outlets, who, out of complicity or ignorance, broadcast them. Landes has collected a significant body of such footage to document the phenomenon.

As in the case of the Jenin "massacre," the al-Durrah affair deepened the distrust between the international press—particularly the European—and the IDF. Behind the scenes in Israel a debate developed about how to treat Charles Enderlin, the correspondent who originally aired the footage on French television. A motion to revoke Enderlin's press credentials in Israel did arise, but it was squelched. The reasons for continuing to permit Enderlin to broadcast are unclear. They likely reflect legal concerns and the practical consideration that direct confrontation with a significant European media figure will only backfire, leading to accusations that Israel is using heavy-handed tactics to manipulate the press.

Israeli spokesmen have displayed a visible discomfort with the al-Durrah affair. Initially, Israeli army officials said that the bullets "apparently" came from Israeli positions and apologized, thereby lending credibility to the story. A subsequent military investigation, however, came to the conclusion that it was "quite plausible that the boy was hit by Palestinian bullets in the course of an exchange of fire." This investigation itself stirred controversy within Israel and caused the Israeli Chief of Staff to distance himself from its proceedings. The Israeli Foreign Ministry similarly showed discomfort with the issue and reportedly concluded that continued discussion was counterproductive and recommended dropping the issue altogether, no matter how strong the exculpatory evidence. Regardless of Israeli officialdom's discomfiture, private individuals continued their quest for answers. Their efforts eventually led David Seaman, the Director of the Israeli government's press office, to endorse the view that the entire episode was staged by the cameraman Talal Abu Rahma. However, no sooner had Seaman expressed his view than another government spokesperson, Miri Eisen, stated that Israel had no position on the staged nature of events and that Seaman's views regarding the staged nature of the event were his personal opinions. Despite this declaration of neutrality Eisen did affirm that Israel was not responsible for al-Durrah's death.[9]

The tortuous road from apology to denial of responsibility highlights the dilemma that the IDF faces when confronted with accusations of civilian casualties. The accusation itself, if plausible, has an immediate political impact. If the truth contradicts the initial headline it will come out in such a delayed and diluted form as to have only a minimal impact on the political process.

The Gaza Beach Incident: The NGO-Media Nexus

On June 9, 2006 an explosion took place on a stretch of beach in Gaza that killed seven members of a picnicking family and reportedly wounded many others. In the aftermath of the incident a young girl, Huda Ghaliya, was filmed mourning over the body of her father. As in the case of Muhammad al-Durrah, the images of a suffering child immediately spread through the global media that evoked widespread sympathy. Although Professor Richard Landes and others raised questions regarding the spontaneity of the film footage, no one doubts that an explosion did take place and that Huda Ghaliya's family members were killed and injured as a result. Three of the wounded were treated in Israel. The controversial questions were whether or not it was an Israeli shell that caused the deaths, and, if so, was it fired, as Palestinian sources claimed, while the Ghaliya family was picnicking? As in earlier cases, the first response by the IDF was to accept responsibility for the incident.

Several days after the event an IDF investigation into the matter concluded that all Israeli shells fired at the time of the picnic were accounted for and that none could have caused injury to the Ghaliya family. Tests on a piece of shrapnel removed in an Israeli hospital from one of the wounded were not consistent with any Israeli shells fired on that day. When Israel's Defense Minister and the Chief of Staff held a press conference to publicize the findings of the investigation, their claims of Israeli innocence were immediately questioned by Human Rights Watch who argued that evidence collected by its "researchers and many independent journalists on the ground in Gaza indicates that the civilians were killed within the time period of the shelling."[10] The disagreement between Human Rights Watch and the Israelis was reported widely in the international press with the testimony of the NGO treated as a neutral observer.[11]

The role that Human Rights Watch played in the aftermath of the Gaza beach explosion was indicative a growing trend in the international media to use of testimony from humanitarian organizations as a reliable source for news. This development poses a serious challenge to the legitimacy of IDF statements. Some in Israel believe that as a rule the NGO community is biased against Israel and, in the words of NGO Watch, an organization founded to monitor the perceived bias of these groups, "focus overwhelmingly on condemning Israel" while "giving minimal attention to Israeli human rights and casualties."[12] Under the cover of non-partisan humanitarian work, so the argument goes, the NGOs pursue a policy of political opposition to Israel. Regardless of whether one agrees with this assessment there is no doubt that a large number of NGOs often criticize IDF policies, cast doubt on its motives and findings, and call for independent investigations into war crimes allegations. Their increasing presence in the media insures that the Israeli government narrative will always be subjected to a harsh audit and that the civilian-victim narrative will resonate deeply in the Western public debate.

The Rise of the Strategic Narrative

The Jenin, Muhammad al-Durrah, and Gaza Beach episodes define the essential parameters of the Civilian-Victims Dilemma: Military operations will immediately spark claims (accurate, exaggerated, and fraudulent) of civilian suffering; the media and the internet will spread these claims globally; third parties will validate the claims; and, consequently, the legitimacy of the operation will be called into question at home, among important allies, and among key target audiences in the area of operations.

The central nature of the adversaries' narrative has emerged as a key element in the information battle. The important information dynamics of battle is changing rapidly due to the global communications revolution. The general impact of this revolution on relations between government and media was described well by British Prime Minister Tony Blair in a speech that he delivered shortly before resigning from office.[13] Technological change, he argued, has let loose a torrent of information which places unprecedented pressure on government officials. "A vast aspect of our jobs today," Blair said, "is coping with the media, its sheer scale, weight and constant hyperactivity." The highly-competitive communications environment has led, in Blair's view, to six major consequences:

1) The lines between news and opinion are now hopelessly blurred, with factual reporting routinely packaged together with political commentary.

2) More air and column space is now devoted to pure commentary, even when presented forthrightly as opinion, than to news itself.

3) The press, fearful of missing out on the most important story of the moment, hunts in a pack.

4) It devotes more attention to stories that produce an immediate emotional impact than to those that offer deep insight. Scandal and controversy which angers and shocks will win over the story that informs and engages the public's intellect.

5) Misconduct grabs more attention than errors of judgment therefore mistakes by officials will inevitably be depicted as products of base motives or, even worse, of conspiracies.

6) Balance has been lost—"things, people, issues, stories are all black and white. Life's usual grey is almost entirely lost."

The phenomenon of the fog of war is well-known. From a military point of view, Blair's six consequences constitute the "noise of war", which is part of that fog. In this frenetic information age, statements from the podium and by multiple other means must provide clarity and be amplified through this fog. To ensure that the military's message is heard and understood requires a comprehensive approach. For the sake of discussion, this approach will be called a "Strategic Narrative," which is a set of integrative policies and processes that tell the military's story—to global audiences. In "telling" this story, words are important, but actions speak louder than words. It is not enough that we avoid harming civilians; we must be seen as making the effort to do so. The Strategic Narrative, therefore, is not simply a public affairs responsibility even though public affairs are certainly key participants. It is the *story* that our actions, words and images all tell together and it is the *process* by which we ensure that actions and words are integrated together so as to achieve our strategic goals. A close examination of hybrid threat communications show that their words are echoes of the actions they plan to take or have taken.

Although the concept of Strategic Narrative is not a recognized term in the American and Israeli military lexicon it is nonetheless a helpful construct in attempting to understand the complex of information problems that democratic armies face in a Hybrid War. It is also useful in analyzing the totality of information challenges that the Israelis encountered in the Second Lebanon War as well as the remedies that they developed in its aftermath. The Second Lebanon war is, in fact, a case study in the failure to develop a Strategic Narrative. Israel's Operation CAST LEAD represents a significant step toward developing one.

For the purpose of this paper, the definition of a Strategic Narrative is a succinct and easily understood description of what a major operation or campaign is intended to achieve. It clarifies the reason for the action, and states the desired outcome or endstate. Although developed to address a specific and significant operational undertaking (e.g. stop Hezbollah from firing missiles from southern Lebanon into northern Israel or to stop the arming of Hamas militias in Gaza), it is developed to inform the global community of the government's intentions and to guide the application and synchronization of national power with that of other coalition or international organizations. It establishes the context and the parameters for all activity in support of the operation or campaign. The narrative is broad but clear (i.e. readily translatable in a variety of languages and cultures) and is informed by the national strategy and policy level guidance associated with a specific mission. The narrative must be approved at the national level and is enduring and inelastic. It is important to note that the enemy has a narrative and, whether it is formal or informal, must be addressed within our narrative's story.

The Second Lebanon War: A Battle of Strategic Narratives

Playing to Hezbollah's Strengths

Hezbollah's self-image can be summed up in a single word: "Resistance." Syrian dictator Bashar al-Asad, one of Hezbollah's strongest allies, recently identified Resistance as "a culture." Whether it makes sense to analyze it as culture, it certainly deserves to be labeled an ideology. The Resistance ideology depicts its adherents as the true defenders of all that is authentic in Arab and Muslim society. Hezbollah labors intensely to project an image of stout-hearted, selfless men dedicated to sacrificing themselves for the greater good. They are agents of renewal purifying Arab and Muslim society while "resisting" the Zionists and those in the Arab world who support them or otherwise benefit from their policies.

Though Israel has superior weaponry, Hezbollah argues, it is suffering from a spiritual and moral crisis. Hassan Nasrallah, the charismatic leader of Hezbollah, interpreted the Israeli withdrawal from southern Lebanon in 2000 as a clear indication of this weakness. In contrast to Hezbollah, Israel cannot sustain casualties and does not have a stomach for a fight. It has, Nasrallah famously said, "a nuclear weapon and the strongest air force in the region, but in truth, it is weaker than a spider's web."[14]

Hezbollah zealously guards its image. Unlike democratic Israel it is not subjected to the harsh audit of a free press and a competitive political process. It wields considerable instruments of intimidation within Lebanon and it has been known to insist that the foreign press, in order to maintain access to the country, treat it without criticism. As part of its post-war image-maintenance exercise, Nasrallah announced a "Divine Victory" over Israel in 2006, playing on the David-versus-Goliath image of a few thousand dedicated youths, blessed by God, holding back the strongest army in the Middle East. Nasrallah's Divine Victory propaganda drew sustenance from the orgy of self-recrimination into which the Israeli polity conducted after the war.

There is good reason to believe that behind the scenes Nasrallah and his followers arrived at a more sober assessment of their achievements than their Divine Victory rhetoric lets on. In his first interview after the ceasefire, Nasrallah admitted having been surprised by Israel's reaction to Hezbollah's kidnapping operation that July and he all but apologized by stating that "we did not believe, even by one percent, that the captive operation would result in such a wide-scale war, as such a war did not take place in the history of wars. Had we known that the captive operation would result in such a war we would not have carried it out at all."[15] Privately Nasrallah may be acknowledging to himself that his miscalculation diminished his personal legitimacy in Lebanon. Additionally, UN Security Council Resolution 1701 constrained Hezbollah's military movement in the south of the country. Add to this the fact that a very significant number—possibly more than 500—of his frontline troops were killed in the Second Lebanon War he provoked. Hundreds of rocket launchers and many millions of dollars' worth of military equipment were destroyed and countless numbers of supporters were left homeless. The list of losses goes on.

And yet, one can't help but think that the Israelis could have done more to strip the veneer from the Divine Victory. One view would argue that the best way to have done so would have been to have won the war unambiguously. Operational success is the greatest propaganda of all. Following that line of reasoning, Israel's general strategic failure in the war is the best explanation as to why Nasrallah emerged from the conflict with his reputation still intact. This is certainly a powerful argument as there is absolutely no denying that a clear Israeli victory would have harmed Nasrallah's image. Nevertheless, when analyzing Israel's strategic failure, the absence of linkage to political warfare, distinct from its combat operations, is also striking. A powerful Strategic Narrative cannot steal victory from the jaws of defeat, but it can highlight certain facts, mask others, and ensure that crucial information is heard above the "noise of war." In short, it can influence perceptions of gain and loss.

Israel's internal Winograd Commission and a number of recent studies have highlighted three factors that account for Israel's general strategic failure:

(1) The political echelon in the government failed to define achievable military goals that, once realized, could readily translate into political gains.

(2) The military leadership placed mistaken confidence in the ability of air power to demoralize and defeat the enemy.

(3) The army was ill-trained and equipped for a ground combat and demonstrated an unexpected lack of discipline.

These three factors each played directly to strengths of Nasrallah's Strategic Narrative. For their part, the Israelis never managed to put together a narrative that might have blunted the power of Hezbollah's political warfare and that could have unified all actions and messages.

War Goals

It is often said of groups like Hezbollah that if they don't lose, they win—and their mere survival is victory. This assessment is based on the notion that in a contest between David and Goliath, the victory of Goliath is fully expected, so any draw goes to the challenger. There is much truth to this assessment, but it is not a good guide for making policy in a Hybrid War context because it diverts attention from the fact that complete annihilation of the enemy is not a realistic outcome. The hybrid enemy will almost always survive in some form to fight another day. The determination of who won and who lost, therefore, will always be, to a certain extent, a matter of perception. The United States Army and the IDF both have a strong interest in managing these perceptions. To paraphrase Osama bin Laden, there is a tendency in the world to back a strong horse. If the power of our adversaries is perceived to be on the rise, then influential third parties, whose support is crucial to our ultimate success, will be more inclined to work with them.

In a world of instantaneous global communication the process of deciding whether or not (or how) to escalate a conflict must include systematic consideration of the battle over perceptions. In the Second Lebanon War it was the Israelis who decided to change the rules of the game, at least as they had existed for the previous six years, between Hezbollah and Israel. This initiative gave Israel the ability to determine ahead of time what would constitute success and how to broadcast it. The messages that the Israeli government enunciated, however, inadvertently were in Nasrallah's favor by setting unreachable goals.

On July 19, 2006, in a major speech before the Knesset, Israeli Prime Minister Olmert defined the objectives of the conflict[16]:

(1) The return of the hostages.

(2) A complete cease fire.

(3) Deployment of the Lebanese army into all of southern Lebanon.

(4) Expulsion of Hezbollah from the area and fulfillment of United Nations Resolution 1559.

By the time the war ended in August only two of these goals—the second and the third—could plausibly be claimed to have been achieved by Israel. Because the fulfillment of UN Resolution 1559 calls for the complete disarmament of all militias this fourth goal amounts to the complete self-annihilation of Hezbollah as a fighting force which was not a possibility. In addition, most of the stated goals were diplomatic and political in nature by requiring the cooperation of Hezbollah, the international community, or the Lebanese government—or some combination of the three.

The Israeli government thus placed into the hands of third parties, none of whom had any interest in an Israeli victory, the keys for creating the perception of a mission successfully accomplished. In an ideal world the Israeli government would have defined goals that were solely dependent on the action of their own forces.

The world, of course, is never ideal. It was probably a mix of factors that pushed the Olmert government to overreach. These likely included a military miscalculation regarding the efficacy of air power, a desire to spur the international community to fulfill its obligations, and, in the case of the hostages, a political and moral imperative to demonstrate continued concern for the suffering of captured soldiers and their families. It is difficult for any leader to deploy massive force without enunciating goals to the public and the military that appear commensurate with the effort. Understandable as the Olmert's government's calculations were, the fact remains that, in the battle for the perception of victory, the Olmert government ceded valuable ground at the outset of the war.

The most that a democratic army can demand of its political leaders is that they take into consideration all relevant factors and then make a determination about how to proceed. It is possible that Olmert did take into consideration the full implications of the goals that he chose. However, from the existing literature there is no reason to believe that the IDF placed before their prime minister the considerations regarding the information battle with Hezbollah. Had the IDF been working with the concept of Strategic Narrative it might well have done so.

Lebanese State Responsibility or the Iranian Division?

Between 12 and 29 July, 2006 the Israeli government demonstrated confusion between two separate information strategies. A report by the Israeli State Comptroller on Public Diplomacy refers to these as "the Lebanese state-responsibility" and "the Iranian-division" strategies. The former stressed the responsibility of the Lebanese state for attacks on Israel emanating from Lebanese territory and the latter depicted Hezbollah as a division of the Iranian army.

Prime Minister Olmert's immediate remarks on July 12 in reaction to the Hezbollah cross-border raid were apparently based the Lebanese state-responsibility strategy, which was an idea that had incubated in Israeli military circles in the years prior to the conflict. At a press conference after a meeting with Prime Minister Koizumi of Japan, Olmert said the following:

> I want to make it clear: This morning's events were not a terrorist attack but the action of a sovereign state that attacked Israel for no reason and without provocation. The Lebanese government, of which Hezbollah is a member, is trying to undermine regional stability. Lebanon is responsible and Lebanon will bear the consequences of its actions."[17]

Five days later, however, when defining the war goals, the Prime Minster adopted a very different tone toward Lebanon. He depicted it as a victim of Syrian and Iranian meddling:

> On the contrary, stability and tranquility in Lebanon, free of the rule of foreign powers, and in the Palestinian Authority, are in Israel's interest. . . . The campaign we are engaged in these days is against the terror organizations operating from Lebanon and Gaza. These organizations are nothing but "sub-contractors" operating under the inspiration, permission, instigation and financing of the terror-sponsoring and peace-rejecting regimes, on the Axis of Evil which stretches from Tehran to Damascus. Lebanon has suffered heavily in the past, when it allowed foreign powers to gamble on its fate.[18]

According to the Comptroller's Report it was not until 29 July, a full twelve days after Olmert's speech, that the IDF itself adopted the new approach.

The abrupt shift to rhetoric regarding the "Axis of Evil" no doubt resulted from the fact that the international community—the United States in particular—was highly supportive of the Siniora government. In addition, as the military later admitted, the Lebanese state-responsibility strategy simply did not correspond to the most obvious aspects of the situation—namely, "that the fighting took place against Hezbollah as an organization and not against Lebanon as a state. The change to the strategy of presenting Hezbollah as an Iranian division came too late to have any benefit."[19]

The differences between the two strategies go to the heart of the importance of developing a Strategic Narrative. As noted, the state-responsibility strategy was based on the inaccurate premise that the Lebanese government actually wielded sufficient power and influence to discipline Hezbollah. If the Israelis truly believed this premise then their messaging was based on a misperception. If they did not believe it—and presumably they did not—then their rhetoric was disingenuous. When combined with a bombing campaign that included considerable targeting of civilian infrastructure, as well as the dislocation of thousands of Lebanese from the south, this Israeli government rhetoric made it sound as if their campaign was targeting all of the Lebanese rather than solely Hezbollah. In doing so, Israel reinforced Hezbollah's long-established civilian-victim narrative.

The Lebanon war brought to light a fundamental division in the Middle East between two rival alliance systems that remain in effect. On one side, Iran leads "the Resistance Coalition" that includes Syria, Hezbollah, and Hamas. It receives some diplomatic and propaganda support from Qatar, the emirate where the influential Al Jazeera news network is based. On the other side of the divide stand the primary supporters of the US order in the Middle East: Saudi Arabia, Egypt, Jordan and the UAE. The conflict between Israel and Hezbollah/Hamas is a wedge issue between the two blocs. The Saudi-Egyptian coalition stands to benefit from Israel defeating Hezbollah and weakening Hamas, but, due to concerns over domestic public opinion, it lacks the ideological resources to advertise this position openly. Iran has a vested interest in exploiting the tension between the Arab states and their societies by heating up the Arab-Israeli conflict. Iran also reaps huge profits from any rise in the price of oil, its sole export, caused by these outbreaks of fighting.

It is politically dangerous for the Saudis and the Egyptians to appear to be supporting the Israelis in wartime. In the information realm, however, they can—and do—deliver messages that indirectly support some Israeli war aims. These messages focus on issues such as Arab self-interest in the face of Iranian (Persian) expansionism and the dangers that the extremism of Hezbollah (and Hamas) pose to the region, etc. The "Iranian division" strategy, therefore, if conducted in a nuanced fashion, had the potential to serve as a basis for the Arabs and Israelis to conduct mutually-reinforcing information programs without actually working together directly.

Arab fears of Iran hegemony represented a concrete benefit for Israel during the Second Lebanon War. A close analysis of the diplomacy would reveal that the Europeans—with the Blair and Merkel governments in the lead—were not as eager to compel the Israelis to adopt a cease-fire as one might have expected from European press reporting. The position of Saudi Arabia and Egypt likely played a role here, too. When the fighting began both Arab states held Hezbollah responsible as both had an interest in seeing Hezbollah defeated.

Had they been more hostile to Israel, then the Europeans would have been treated to immediate and unrelenting pressure from the Arab world to take diplomatic action against Israel. Unfortunately the contradictions and sharp shifts in Israel's public diplomacy meant that the Israelis were not in a position to exploit this factor to its fullest potential.

The Information Battle

The confusion in Israel's public diplomacy showed that it did not have a systematic and strategic vision for prosecuting the information battle. At the same time Israel's air-war strategy generated powerful images that appeared to validate Hassan Nasrallah's "spider web" theory while also providing copious material for Hezbollah's civilian-victim narrative.

Hezbollah's information apparatus was fully prepared to exploit the images of Israel's air war. Through the use of heavy-handed minders and threats of revoking access to the press, Hezbollah worked to manage the flow of images and reports out of Lebanon with shockingly successful results. It forbade, for instance, the media to publish photos of its own fighters and it gave almost no interviews. This discipline of the organization was impressive. It was also unreported by the striking compliance of the international press corps. The press would never quietly respect such ground rules from any western country, much less Israel. "Throughout the conflict," Marvin Kalb wrote in a perceptive study of the subject, "the rarest picture of all was that of a Hezbollah guerrilla. It was as if the war on the Hezbollah side was being fought by ghosts."[20] The non-existence of Hezbollah's combat imagery influenced perceptions in three important ways:

(1) It fostered the impression that, on one side, stood a modern army and on the other only civilians.

(2) It subtly undercut Israel's claim that Hezbollah used civilians as human shields—if there are no pictures of fighters then there can be no proof of fighters exploiting helpless civilians.

(3) It removed the Syrian and Iranian influence from the scene.

To be successful, Israel's information activities must spotlight a well-hidden fact: in Lebanon the Israeli army is fighting against the very best training and equipment that the modern *Iranian* military establishment can muster. The imagery of the war simply did not tell this story. Even under the best of circumstances the "Iranian division" role is more difficult to explain as it is less compelling than the civilian-victim narrative and it cannot be captured in images by the media. By contrast, the destruction wrought by Israel in Lebanon was something tangible that the international press corps could taste, touch, see, and smell and was consequently easier to show or describe.

As a consequence, over time, the theme of "disproportionality" crept in to almost all media coverage on the war. "No theme," writes Kalb, "resonated through the coverage of the Lebanese war more forcefully than the repeated assertion by Arab and Western reporters that Israel responded "disproportionately" to Hezbollah's initial provocation."[21] Before long, concern over disproportionality moved from television screens to the halls of the diplomats. Pressure mounted on Israel to accept a ceasefire and on the United States to pressure its ally to halt its operation. The concern over disproportionality, therefore, has direct military implications. In order for the IDF to gain lasting benefit from its operations it must have enough time to achieve its essential goals. The harder the IDF strikes, the faster the diplomatic pressure grows and the less opportunity it has, requiring a high-tempo operation from its outset.

The main theme of Hezbollah's message—Lebanese civilian casualties— was reinforced not just by the media, but, as one should now expect, also the testimony from human rights organizations. For instance on 2 August, Human Rights Watch issued a report accusing the Israelis of "serious violations of international humanitarian law." According to the report, the IDF had killed such a large number of civilians—who had no apparent connection to military activity—as to suggest that they had been purposefully targeted. The report further argued that the Israeli claim that Hezbollah was using civilians as human shields was unfounded. "Hezbollah occasionally did store weapons in or near civilian homes and fighters placed rocket launchers within populated areas . . . which are serious violations of laws of war . . . [h]owever, those cases do not justify the IDF's extensive use of indiscriminate force . . ."[22]

The rising concern over civilian suffering had a significant impact on diplomatic developments. Two examples of this stand out and will be examined. On 26 July, Secretary of State Condoleezza Rice attended the Rome Conference where, at one dramatic moment, she shared the podium with Lebanese Prime Minister Fouad Siniora who called emotionally for an immediate ceasefire saying that everything that delays it prolongs the suffering of the Lebanese. This encounter must have been more than a little uncomfortable for the American Secretary of State caught publicly beside and between her Israeli and Lebanese allies.

Four days later Rice was in Jerusalem for talks with the Israeli government and scheduled to embark shortly thereafter for Lebanon. Her agenda was disrupted by the Israeli bombardment of a four-story building in the Lebanese city of Qana that killed 28 people. Initial reports called it a "massacre" and put the number of dead much higher. As in past cases, stories of whole families crushed in the rubble immediately hit the media. The resulting outrage forced Rice to postpone her visit to Beirut. The Winograd Commission's final report on the war contains a short but telling summary of Rice's conversation with Olmert, immediately after the Qana event:

> The Prime Minister opened the discussion by saying that the event in the village of Qana was an unfortunate mishap, but it was important to emphasize that 28 rocket attacks on Israel were carried out from the village, and that the population of the village was warned ahead of time that it must leave from there. The Secretary of State responded that, in light of the event, the rules of the game had changed. The parties then proceeded to discuss the issues on the agenda.[23]

That Qana was a potential "game changer" in the view of the US Secretary of State was not lost on Hezbollah and its supporters. They left nothing to chance as members of the foreign press were escorted to the village and the bodies of dead children were displayed in staged rescue and recovery scenes. Enterprising bloggers would eventually prove that many of the photos were staged.[24] Regardless of their ghoulish post-mortem manipulation by Hezbollah, the Lebanese civilians' deaths were real and the bloggers' activities did not diminish the immediate political impact of the imagery.

Authoritarian "Strength" Versus Democratic "Weakness"

In terms of projecting its preferred image to the world, Hezbollah benefits from an unusually high level of secrecy and discipline. It gave no interviews to reporters during the war and benefitted from an effective internal machinery of persuasion and intimidation. This latter feature elicits from the wider Shiite Lebanese society outward signs of support that reinforce Hezbollah's key themes and messages and enhances its operational security. On rare occasions Hezbollah's message machinery becomes visible. In one of its reports on civilian victims of the Second Lebanon War, Human Rights Watch managed to catch two revealing glimpses of Hezbollah's persuasive techniques. In one case, an Israeli air strike on a village demolished the home of a man named Najib and killed him in the process. Unbeknownst to Najib, Hezbollah had enlarged the basement of a neighboring house and used it to store weapons. Believing that he was safe, Najib did not heed Israeli warnings to evacuate his home. When the family learned of what Hezbollah had done, it complained to the organization and demanded compensation. At first, Hezbollah greeted the family's demands with threats and denials. Eventually public opinion in the village shifted toward the family and Hezbollah was forced to be more forthcoming and conciliatory. According to one witness who spoke to Human Rights Watch:

> After the incident, the family had a fight with Hezbollah. At first, Hezbollah denied the allegations, but when the whole town learned of the incident, they finally admitted it. The person they complained to is also in charge of compensation, and he delayed the payment to the family. The family has stopped speaking out because they are afraid they will lose the compensation.[25]

In a separate episode, on the day that the war broke out Hezbollah fighters showed up unexpectedly in the Sunni village of Marwahin, near the Israeli border, to store weapons and engage in other military activities. When a 52-year-old woman named Zahra Abdullah saw fighters storing weapons outside her house, she went to them and begged, "Please, there are kids inside this home." Her pleas fell on deaf ears:

> One of the Hezbollah fighters turned his automatic weapon on Zahra, and told her to "shut up and go inside." Zahra returned to her home, crying. That day, many villagers fled from Marwahin following Israeli orders to evacuate the village. Twenty-three fleeing civilians from Marwahin, including Zahra Abdullah, were killed in an Israeli air strike on their convoy.[26]

Presumably incidents such as these played themselves out all across southern Lebanon during and after the war, though Human Rights Watch does not claim as much. And, presumably, no small amount of resentment toward Hezbollah developed as a result. But, as the incidents themselves suggest, Hezbollah has a set of persuasive tools—ranging from the mobilization of ethnic solidarity, to lying, to paying for support, to outright thuggish intimidation. These allow it to impose on Lebanese society a level of discipline that has no counterpart in a liberal and democratic society such as Israel.

This difference between the two societies carries certain advantages for Hezbollah in the information battle. This fact is most obvious when one compares Nasrallah's "Divine Victory" and its gaudy parades with its Israeli counterpart, the Winograd Commission, a meticulous, painful, and lengthy public postmortem of wartime mistakes by a panel. The Divine Victory campaign, though couched as a celebration, deserves to be understood as a form of public instruction to the Lebanese. To the Shiite supporters of Hezbollah it speaks in the tone addressed to the family of Najib: "Don't break ranks. Criticism of Hezbollah will only be used by our rivals to weaken the entire community." To the Sunnis and Christians, it speaks as the fighters did to Zahra Abdullah: "Shut up! We know what is best for the country." In either case, breaking ranks with Hezbollah or casting open doubt on the Divine Victory carries with it serious risks.

In the information war the single most powerful weapon that the Israelis could theoretically develop would be third-party validators from within Lebanese Shiite society—people who would stand up and credibly challenge the Divine Victory ethos on the basis of Lebanese values. A significant breaking of ranks could do more to tarnish the image of Nasrallah than any flow of information from the outside, especially from Israel. Fostering such a development, however, is extremely difficult for Israel because the forms of interaction with its neighbors are weighted with heavy historical baggage. For the United States Army—as an expeditionary force—the opportunities to develop third-party validators (such as the Sunni tribes in al-Anbar in 2006) are often much greater.

Democratic societies deeply believe that a disciplined process of self-criticism conducted in an environment of open debate is a source of great strength and renewal. In general terms there is no doubt that this is true. In a war of perceptions, however, it is also a stark fact that the absence of public dissent fosters the appearance of strength and unanimity. Conversely, self-criticism appears as weakness and divisiveness. In an age of instantaneous communications, openness can have serious operational implications certainly with respect to perceptions of relative strength and also with respect to operational security.

In the Second Lebanon War the Israelis suffered from both problems of openness and instant communications. Liberal use of cellular telephones and open discussion with the press by soldiers at all levels led to serious leaks of classified information. Hezbollah had the ability to anticipate Israeli actions simply by listening to the media. This open discussion by IDF troops of setbacks, poor planning and other difficulties during combat operations also undermined morale on the Israeli home front while projecting to the enemy an appearance of fecklessness that further hurt their war effort.

Gaza, Lessons Applied

The Missing Strategic Organization

The Winograd Commission dealt only peripherally on what the Israelis call *"Hasbara."* *Hasbara* is a Hebrew noun that means "explanation" but is an all-encompassing Israeli term that, if it existed in the United States system, would be roughly equivalent to an amalgamation of "public diplomacy," "public affairs," and "influence." (For the purposes of this discussion we will translate it as "public diplomacy.") The Commission highlighted the importance of the issue and called for institutional reform but did not delve into it in depth.

In the aftermath of the Second Lebanon War at least two investigative initiatives were launched to examine deficiencies in the public diplomacy system The first was a military inspection team which completed its work in December 2006 and a comprehensive government-wide review conducted by the Office of the State Comptroller which finished its report in January 2007.[27] This effort was preceded by a 2002 Comptroller's report that made recommendations to fix severe deficiencies in the field of *Hasbara*. In the acrimonious political climate in the wake of Israel's withdrawal from southern Lebanon in 2000, this earlier report's recommendations were ignored. Following the 2006 war, however, there was a near-universal awareness of the importance of the information battle.

First and foremost, the Israelis concluded that they lacked a leadership organization for *Hasbara*. With brutal frankness the Comptroller's report pointed to deficiencies resulting from an institutional vacuum. It strongly recommended the creation of an overarching coordinating body vested with sufficient authority to integrate a whole-of-government approach to public diplomacy. The absence of a strategic apparatus had contributed to the lack of strategic concepts and plans. By emphasizing the failure to develop "an overarching concept of public diplomacy with respect to foreign and defense issues" the Comptroller's language made it crystal clear that, in the Israeli conception, public diplomacy is a national security discipline. It is tied intimately to foreign policy, defense, and homeland security policy.[28] It also covers the issues, such as branding and national image that Americans more typically associate with the term "public diplomacy."

The Defense Ministry and the IDF clearly have great respect in Israel's public diplomacy arena. However, the report also makes clear that, during the war, the IDF's public diplomacy efforts sometimes overshadowed those of the rest of the government and determined the national message without adequate coordination with other ministries. This is where democratic governments face their biggest organizational challenge. In the Second Lebanon War some tension reportedly developed between the army and the Foreign Ministry. The latter complained that "although there was close cooperation . . . with the IDF spokesman," that cooperation "had no influence on the formation of the message and the communications policy of the IDF representatives." That policy, the Foreign Ministry stated, was "formulated somewhere else on the basis of independent calculations that did not take into account the suggestions put forward by the Foreign Ministry."[29]

This, too, points to a lack of national leadership that was a key factor in fostering this inter-ministerial tension. In the first weeks of the war, responsibility for coordinating public diplomacy at the national level first fell to the prime minister's Director of Media and Public Affairs, Assaf Shariv, who fulfilled this responsibility in an ad hoc fashion from the start of hostilities on 12 July until 3 August, 2006. The duty then passed to the Government Secretariat, because Shariv was fully engaged as the personal press assistant to the Prime Minister. A marked improvement took place once the Government Secretariat took charge probably because of its normal responsibilities include coordination between the prime minister's office and other branches of government. Despite the improvement, an institutional deficiency remained as evidenced by the fact that the official duties of the Secretariat did not include public diplomacy. That the Secretariat was forced into action in a crisis shows a compelling need for a full-time office dedicated to providing national-level leadership in this area.[30]

In response to the demand throughout the government for a new office, on 8 July, 2007 the Olmert government established the Directorate of National Information in the prime minister's office.[31] "Directorate" is something of a misnomer as the office does not have directive power but rather has responsibility for coordinating the public diplomacy activities of the entire government without stepping on the prerogatives of each of the operational entities—Defense, Foreign Ministry, etc. Though only a coordinator, it does have a seat at the table in the formation of national-level foreign and defense policies so that public diplomacy concerns will not be treated as an afterthought and that issues needing resolution at the national level can receive timely attention. In addition to these responsibilities the office also develops plans and strategies, provides regular guidance for the entire government, and has a lead role in the information effort during national emergencies.[32]

By all accounts, the Directorate of National Information significantly improved inter-ministerial coordination eighteen months later in Operation

CAST LEAD against Hamas. The main impact of the office was to achieve an unprecedented level of Israeli government message discipline. Fully-coordinated political and foreign policy statements—regarding the responsibility of Hamas for the war and the role of Iran in stoking it—were adopted by all ministries and disseminated consistently throughout the conflict. The Directorate also made sure that up-to-the-minute guidance was available to all who needed it. The concept "Strategic Narrative" is not a recognized part of the Israeli national security vocabulary. However, the mere existence of a strategic-level office devoted to public diplomacy and tied closely to the Defense Ministry ensured that the system behaved as if the concept was in fact part of standard operating procedure.

Message Discipline and Closure

The Winograd Commission did not analyze in depth the question of public diplomacy though it devoted considerable attention to the severe problem of classified information finding its way into the media. It pointed out that whereas Hezbollah was very careful to avoid leaks of sensitive information the Israelis were not. Classified policy debates, information regarding military operations, complaints of soldiers in the field—all this and more made its way into the media through a variety of channels. These included liberal cell phone use by soldiers in the field, unregulated contact between officers and members of the press, and intentional leaking for one purpose or another. The Commission's final report stated that leaks to the media actually had operational significance on the field of battle and posed a significant threat to national security. It called for a renewed and sustained effort to fight the culture of leaking. It flatly and pointedly rejected the position of those who believe that due to modern communications there is nothing that can stem the flow information except surrender to the inevitable.

In Operation CAST LEAD, the Israeli government obviously took the Winograd Commission's recommendations to heart. Whereas the information anarchy characterized the Second Lebanon war, "discipline" was the watchword of CAST LEAD. The Israelis sealed off Gaza to the press, tightly regulated the interaction between soldiers and the media, and banned the use of cell phones by the military. There can be little doubt that this policy led to a higher level of operational security than was obtained in Lebanon. The new policies combined with the creation of the Directorate of National Information allowed the Israelis to broadcast a much tighter message than most other democracies have achieved in war.

The power of this message discipline by the Israeli government was enhanced by two other factors. The Israelis made innovative use of social media sites and they created streamlined processes to ensure that information and imagery from the battlefield made it to these sites in a timely fashion. Giving regular soldiers cameras and letting them tell their stories was a highly effective means of enhancing the Strategic Narrative of a democracy at war. Using the internet to disseminate this message allowed Israel to bypass the press which puts its own "spin" on reporting. This bypassing was an especially effective mechanism for speaking directly to trusting audiences such as the Israeli public.

Taken together these policies used in Operation CAST LEAD were successful in three areas. First, with respect to the home audience, some faith was restored in the government and, importantly, in the military itself. After the information debacle of the Second Lebanon War, a major goal—if not *the* goal—of Israeli government information activities was to demonstrate to the Israeli population that the government and military were as efficient and competent as they had been presumed to be before 2006. Second, operational security was vastly enhanced through the plugging of leaks, restriction of the press, and communications security. And third, by sealing off Gaza, the Israelis probably bought enough time to finish their military operation before the diplomatic pressure became unbearable. One way to avoid another Qana is, certainly, to keep reporters out.[33]

With respect to foreign audiences, however, the success of the new policies was much less clear-cut. The message discipline that the Israelis exhibited certainly did not hurt their cause with foreign audiences. However, the benefits were somewhat mitigated by the decision to close Gaza to the international press. When reviewing the tense history of relations between the Israelis and the international media, one cannot help but wonder whether closure was a form of payback for Jenin, Muhammad al-Durrah, the Gaza Beach explosion, etc. The situation suggests that when it came time to argue the case in favor of giving the press access to Gaza the international press corps had few advocates from within the ranks of Israeli officialdom.

Lorenzo Cremonesi, an Italian correspondent for *Corrierre Della Serra* who managed to slip into Gaza during the fighting, commented on the anger of the press corps by arguing that the policy of closure boomeranged on the Israelis. When the press finally did gain access, he explained, they were even more adversarial and in their mood for revenge looked for stories that undermined the Israeli's message. Cremonesi filed reports on a number of subjects that advanced Israel's narrative such as Hamas using ambulances as transport for Hamas guerrillas and leaders, knowing that the IDF would not shoot them, and the intent of Hamas to carry out vendettas against Fatah rather than taking care of the Gazan population. In Cremonesi's view, had Israel opened up Gaza to the European press, it would have seen many more reports of the kind that he produced. The policy was, he said, "a horrible mistake."[34]

The advantages that the Israelis gained from closure of Gaza need to be weighed against the effects, both immediate and long-term, of angering the press. In addition, there also existed an intermediate position, between complete closure and free access, which could have been taken into consideration. When Israel shut the press out, many of the correspondents seem to have had little to do other than to sit outside of Gaza and watch the smoke plumes rise above the horizon. Had Israel provided limited access to Gaza or provided other activities that would have given the press the ability to file interesting reports (the ability to do, that is, the job they were sent to do), it might have mitigated some of the anger that the closure policy engendered. In short, a fully successful Strategic Narrative requires an active press engagement program which the Israelis did not supply.

Perhaps unconsciously, the Israelis in Gaza took a page out of Hezbollah's book when they showed the press only what they wanted it to see while broadcasting their message directly to the world. The international press, however, will use whatever tools are available to it in order to gain access to sources. Hezbollah, being a secretive, authoritarian terrorist organization, is not susceptible to moral suasion or to legal action. It is also intimidating and the press accepted the ground rules that the organization laid down. In Israel, however, the press openly bristled at the restrictions that the Israelis imposed. It took its case to the Israeli Supreme Court and won. The Court actually ordered the IDF to let the media into Gaza. The IDF, however, did not immediately respect the decision on the basis of "temporary security reasons."[35]

It remains to be seen whether in any future operation in Gaza the IDF will be able to shut the press out. One suspects that this policy will not be repeated. Moreover, as a general strategy, closure is only possible in Gaza due to its unique geographic and political setting. Even the IDF would not be able to close off the West Bank and Lebanon to the foreign press.

Israel's and Egypt's closure of Gaza did not prevent Hamas from disseminating its messages. There was one major media outlet with a correspondent in Gaza during the conflict—Al-Jazeera. The closure policy had the inadvertent effect of forcing all other outlets to draw on material from Al-Jazeera which was highly sympathetic to Hamas and broadcast images that supported its civilian-victim narrative. The enhanced role of Al-Jazeera raises the question, in regards to the Civilian-Victim Dilemma, whether closure managed to increase or blunt the power of the Israeli message in any way.

In Gaza, the civilian-victim narrative remained the Achilles heel of the Israeli information battle. Perhaps the most heart-wrenching moment in the war came when a Palestinian doctor from Gaza telephoned an Israeli television news program. Dr. Izzeldin Abuelaish was known as a strong advocate of Israeli-Palestinian reconciliation. He was scheduled to speak, in Hebrew, to an Israeli television reporter with whom he was on friendly terms about the situation in Gaza. Dr. Abuelaish came on the telephone live in a highly anguished state. His three daughters had just been killed by an Israeli attack on his home. And other family members had been wounded. "Why did they do this?" he repeatedly asked. The Israeli television personality was visibly disturbed by the suffering of his friend and could not answer. Nor could Israeli officials.[36]

There can be no doubt that, between Lebanon and Gaza, the Israeli government vastly improved its ability to explain its actions and goals. Their use of web-based vehicles such as YouTube to distribute UAV imagery of, for instance, Hamas fighters loading trucks with rockets was effective with sympathetic audiences. Of course, hostile audiences could view the same content and draw vastly different conclusions from it.

The Israelis have yet to find a formula to convince a skeptical international press corps—and significant segments of Arab and Western public opinion—that the human cost of their military operations is morally justified and that they made every effort to minimize civilian suffering. Whether such a formula exists is a very complex question. Nevertheless, two of the greatest imperatives of the IDF (and of western militaries in general) are to try to find it and, equally important to be seen to be searching for it in the face of a cynical and calculating enemy. Making sure that the world sees the effort exerted to find this formula is of crucial importance. The democratic army's moral strength lies in its inherently deep concern over the value of human life. This concern is a thread that must be woven into the heart of the Strategic Narrative of all western militaries' operations.

Emerging Lessons for the United States Army

Disclaimer

Operation CAST LEAD was very recent to the writing of this chapter and its follow-up remains an ongoing operation. Any conclusions that are drawn at this junction should be considered with a skeptical eye. Additionally there are unique environmental factors that must be understood when viewing the IDF's experience against Hezbollah and Hamas or southern Lebanon and Gaza.

Unique Conditions

(1) Differences between Israel and the United States:

• The United States, as a world power possessing an expeditionary military, has greater ability to work "by, with, and through" indigenous forces—a fact which gives the US much greater latitude in terms of developing local allies and work with regionally partners towards common objectives.

• Due to differences of size, law, and policy, the United States does not have (and probably never will have) a position comparable to the Israelis' National Information Directorate; therefore the military, when seeking timely and authoritative national-level guidance, must use other mechanisms.

• The IDF see these operations as one of a series of limited objective operations. The military, through its operations, set the conditions for their political leadership to negotiate from a position of strength. The US in contrast develops campaigns that have an enduring endstate. The concepts of campaigns and strategies that involve unified action are part of a comprehensive campaign that brings with it allies, coalitions, and regional partners.

(2) Second Lebanon War:

• The IDF attempted to achieve ground success through a strategic air campaign. When it committed ground forces it did so without surprise or sufficient force and was hampered by a number of operational and strategic constraints.

• The IDF view of their persistent conflict as a series of limited objective military operations or campaigns.

(3) Gaza:

• The IDF had almost total control of the border surrounding Gaza with the exception of that with Egypt. The Egyptian government made significant attempts to close the border using para-military forces.

• The IDF barred reporters from the area with the exception of Al Jazerra reporters and stringers reporting from within the territory.

• The ground forces made a limited incursion into Gaza and did not occupy.

Insights

The following insights are based on emerging lessons that we can only surmise at this point. More study and comparison is required, especially in the area of information strategies and potential effectiveness.

• Civilians become cultural, religious, and ideological weapons when the US is attacking enemies who come from a culture that is different from ours. The gap between the attacker and attacked is so great that no amount of explanation and reparations can compensate.

• Full spectrum operations in the information age requires a comprehensive approach to information operations to create greater understanding between people and organizations and to advance mission success. Every line of effort must combine words, deeds, and images carefully crafted to elicit the desired behavior of every group whose behavior matters to accomplishing the mission.

• Human populations are the central feature and principle operational consideration in any conflict context. Human populations on varying scales are the ultimate arbiters of the success or failure of military operations—military forces cannot hope to achieve lasting results without the participation of relevant publics. This necessitates working "by, with, and through" relevant actors and publics.

• Cultural fluency developed by interacting with and understanding relevant populations and engaging them with coordinated programs, plans, themes, messages, images, and products synchronized with the other actions taken to achieve lasting results.

• Deterrence is a function of both perceptions and military potential. Persistent engagement is required to establish a dialogue to develop enduring relationships that may deter escalation and reduce conflict.

• Non-state actors will use the tactic of using human shields as a means of countering their conventional weakness and Islamist extremist movements will do so as an ideological goal by seeking to push populations into the war on their side.

• If international legitimacy is desired, an effort has to be made to convince key allies and international organizations of the legal and just nature of the operations based on the values and perceptions of those critical audiences.

• A comprehensive information strategy is an essential element of any campaign or major operation as part of the design phase and a by-product is the strategic or operational narrative. This narrative establishes the context and the parameters for all activity in support of the operation or campaign.

• If possible, a force should avoid engaging an asymmetric enemy on the enemy's own terms. Conversely, the enemy should not be allowed to seize and retain the information high ground—such as cyberspace. The Internet should not be ceded "enemy-held territory" from which to transmit his message.

• The media is one of an asymmetric enemy's most effective weapons—TV, print, internet, radio, street leaflets, DVDs and video games, etc. Hezbollah's information motto could be summed up in the words: "If you haven't captured it on film you haven't fought."

• An asymmetric enemy will plan and calculate operations for its psychological impact and the exploitation of the images/videos for an advantage across multiple media (new and traditional). Asymmetric enemies can conduct successful information activities or strategy by:

▪ Employing experts specializing in psychological warfare, propaganda and use of new media tools.

▪ Operating media outlets and employing a foreign relations unit.

▪ Near real-time video reporting of civilian and enemy casualties, often staging events for a media effect or bating operations for the US to cause innocent casualties.

▪ Not reporting its own casualties and hiding among the innocent civilians to prevent determination.

▪ Performing expert editing and manipulation of photos and videos and timely transmission to the media to present a false picture to gain regional and international sympathy—"fauxtography."[37]

▪ Take advantage of questionable journalistic ethics and standards in order to be first to report.

▪ Cyberspace is both a combat multiplier and allows them to conduct economy of force mission on a strategic scale.

An Initial Review of the Implications

An initial assessment of the Israeli experience allows us to draw tentative institutional implications. Aptly, several of the observations link directly to findings developed in support of the Strategic Communications Joint Integrating Concept (JIC). Although not an all inclusive list, the following describes focal points for further exploration in conjunction with assessments of contemporary operations and experimentation venues.

Policy

- The lack of a National Strategy related to strategic influence impedes the Department of Defense and military services in operationalizing the key enablers.

- National level policies and their underlying legal authorities related to public affairs, psychological operations, and strategic communications are outdated, they still draw distinctions between audiences—distinctions that have been obviated by the ongoing revolution in information technology and human connectedness.

- Centralize Strategic (Operational) Narrative development and promulgation as a method to enable unified action.

- Continue to promote decentralize approval authority of themes, messages and supporting products as an important way to generate tempo in information engagement activities.

- Empower commander's at the lowest level through mission type orders to engage, communicate and collaborate with key actors and audiences with the authority to amplify and clarify actions across multiple forms of appropriate media.

- Use of media embeds as a routine means of maintaining transparency and credibility that supports our narrative and negate the adversary narratives.

- Implement a comprehensive information-sharing policy within the DOD and with other USG departments and agencies in order to achieve the level of understanding of potential foreign audiences and the integration of information tasks.

- Continue to develop streamlined, rapid declassification and release procedures for intelligence and combat camera visual information (VI) media that have strategic effect. These continue to provide compelling evidence that often negates the adversaries' propaganda.

Concepts and Doctrine

• Consider development of a long-term theater specific information engagement plan which identifies short-, mid- and long-term objectives, enduring themes, common conduits, routine engagement opportunities, and provides guidance, direction, milestones and means of measurement.

• Synchronizing information engagement themes, messages, images and actions across the force with more traditional Army operations will be increasingly critical to mission accomplishment and the achievement of enduring results.

• Create an independent Functional Concept for information engagement alongside the existing Functional Concepts.

• Shift the institutional focus from the "Commander's Intent"—the commander's vision of how he wants conditions on the ground at the conclusion of the operations; to the "Commander's Narrative"—a hybrid concept that includes how the commander wants conditions on the ground at the conclusion of operations, but also makes explicit how the commander wants the operation to unfold in the infosphere—shaping how the events will be perceived.

• Develop staff procedures for rapid assessment of friendly and enemy information strategies.

• Establish collaborative processes for integrating information engagement activities with nonmilitary entities.

• Include information engagement instructions in the main body (coordinating instructions) portion of the operations order or plan: detailed instructions for specific disciplines whose primary function supports information engagement, such as psychological operations, public affairs or combat camera, could remain in current annexes and appendices.

• Developing procedures for ensuring timely release authority and dissemination of information products. Decentralize the approval process to facilitate rapid reaction to events that are locally attuned.

- Importance of using the operations security (OPSEC) process to mitigate risk during the planning of operations and continued assessments of the program that protect the mission and the force during execution.

- Importance of adopting the strategic or operational narrative as a mechanism for bringing coherence to actions, images and words.

- Integration of Human Terrain Teams (HTT) and social-cultural-political mapping into battle command systems and the Information Engagement planning and assessment process.

Organization

- Information engagement must be elevated from one of the five Army information tasks to a warfighting function alongside fires, intelligence, maneuver, and the rest in order to elevate its importance in Army operations and to ensure its activities are not conceived through the lens of other warfighting functions.

- Consider establishment of a standing Army Information Engagement Analysis and Response Element to preempt prepare for and respond to propaganda, misinformation and disinformation.

- Increase psychological and computer network operations capacity to support information engagement operations within indigenous audiences, tactical level is ever increasing more important for mission success.

- Increase combat camera capacity to ensure that Information Engagement is available to support information engagement requirements at the lowest level.

- Integrate Foreign Area Officers (FAO) representatives into operational and possibly tactical staffs.

Training

• Institutionalize the incorporation of information tasks into training exercises (individual and collective). Include the information aspects of the operational environment as part of "conditions" of training.

• Institutionalize programs to educate, train, and develop soldiers and leaders who can confidently and effectively engage, communicate (includes active listening), collaborate, and otherwise interact with relevant publics and actors in a manner that creates an operational advantage to accomplish the mission.

• Train all soldiers, leaders and staffs in the new doctrinal techniques and procedures of leader/soldier engagement.

• Establish digital VI (visual information) media gunnery to train novice combat arms soldiers on combat camera skills necessary to support information engagement VI media exploitation and forensic documentation.

• Integration with "soft" programs working on the ground who can conduct assessments of root causes, activities, information products and efforts; establish interagency 360 degree plan-execute-assess system.

• Emphasis on OPSEC training by all soldiers, staffs, and units.

• Develop stronger linkage vice stove-piping of the NETWAR/NETOPS community with the Information Engagement (IE) community of practice.

• Expand training in the most universally applicable new forms of media and communication. Training at all levels should be devoted to the subject of, and offered through the tools available in new media and Internet-based outreach, including blogging, social networks and video-sharing web sites. Emphasis on strategies for outreach using these new forms of communication must become more central to Army education.

• Enhanced language training—both linguistic and cultural—including public speaking, media strategies, presentation skills in new media, and web-based communication as well as cultural literacy, including more options for in-country language training, should be a much higher priority for the Army.

• Enculturation should become a priority throughout the Army's educational processes. Enculturation is the process by which a person learns the requirements of the culture by which he or she is surrounded, and acquires values and behaviors that are appropriate or necessary in that culture. If successful, enculturation results in competence in the language, values and rituals of the culture.

Materiel

• Develop and make training aide support packages available to support both collective and individual training requirements.

• Developing visual battle command system technologies to represent dynamic social networks.

• Develop technologies to help track and visually represent the propagation and mutation of messages/actions through a social communication system.

• Provide reach back to necessary communication or cultural expertise.

• Develop modeling and simulation to approximate the likely effects of signals on the attitudes and behaviors of various audiences. Consider the development of simulations and models to analyze and graphically represent dynamic social networks as well as ascertain the effects of engagements with selected publics and actors. Use live, virtual and constructive training domains as test beds for these capabilities and spiral develop them into the force.

• Develop standardized combat camera kits and supporting network systems across the force that allows ease and timely capture and exchange of VI media. Provide kits to all combat arms forces to support information engagement.

• Provide technologies to identify capture and translate large volumes of audio, video and textual information and alert analysts to specific portions that indicate potential interest.

• Develop interoperable, scalable and tailor-able information infrastructures to support flexible information sharing across organizations and cultures.

• Provide rapid visual imagery acquisition and transmission capability throughout the force, from the soldier on patrol to UAS (unmanned aircraft systems) or robotic sensors in support.

• Bridge the IE effort in the field with capabilities and more direct and responsive reach-back.

Leader Development and Education

• Develop an Army culture that embraces engagement.

• Institutionalize programs to educate, train, and develop soldiers and leaders who can confidently and effectively engage, communicate, collaborate, and otherwise interact with relevant publics and actors that create an operational advantage toward mission accomplishment.

• Develop early understanding and exchanges among media experts and Army leaders at lower levels (Army Captain Career Courses and Advanced Non-Commission Officers Courses).

• Familiarize and educate military personnel in information task disciplines to build a more comprehensive understanding of each mission area's capabilities and limitations.

• Developing an understanding of the importance and application of information as a battlefield function should be institutionalized throughout the Army.

• Incorporate the principles of IE into the core curricula of professional military schools, with varying levels of emphasis depending on the level of the school.

• Develop leaders who have the knowledge, skills and aptitude to connect actions, words and images in a decentralized environment.

• Implement a long range information training strategy.

• Augment interagency education with IE planning in order to break down the walls, reduce misperceptions, and build confidence and synergy required for planning and integration.

Personnel

• Increase numbers of linguists and foreign area officers and potentially expand the field to include warrant officers and non-commissioned officers.

• Increase number VI media specialists and combat camera (COMCAM) soldiers to support tactical level units (down to battalion level).

• Consider significant use of nonmilitary personnel in the form of advisors, contractors, etc. in order to gain the necessary expertise in some information areas—with implications for hiring, contracting and budgeting.

• Establish dedicated OPSEC planning and assessment specialists to manage the process and programs for the commander.

• Establish career incentives that reward language and foreign-area skills and specialties.

Facilities

- Commit resources to Combat Training Centers (CTCs) and other collective training environments to routinely exercise information tasks.

- Support the creation of an "influence range," an information engagement training facility focused on training social-cultural engagements across live, constructive and virtual training environments.

Conclusion

Since the 1973 war the IDF has not engaged in major state-to-state war. From time to time, conflict in Lebanon has resulted in limited engagements between the IDF and elements of the Syrian military, but these cannot be truly defined as wars. For more than thirty years, the Israelis have found themselves, instead, in a state of persistent conflict with terrorist enemies using techniques of irregular warfare.

Conflict with states, however, has not ended. Iran and Syria have strong interests, rooted in their regional ambitions, in perpetuating conflict between Israel and its neighbors. For a variety of reasons, they have found that the most effective method of stoking the fires is to build up proxies, Hamas and Hezbollah being the two most important ones. The aid that these two organizations receive from Syria and Iran, in the form of training, equipment, resources, and diplomatic and propaganda support, has imbued them with state-like qualities. As a result, "normal" wars for Israel are Hybrid Wars.

The advent of the Hybrid War era coincides with two global developments: the end of the Cold War and the mass communications revolution. Both of these have profoundly altered the strategic, political, and moral contexts in which Israel faces off against its enemies. During the Cold War, Israel carried out fixed-piece tank battles with Syria and Egypt, who were Soviet client states. The West, as a whole, perceived that it had a profound stake in the success of Israeli combined arms.

In the last thirty years, many in the West are no longer as convinced, as they were during the Cold War that they have a stake in an Israeli victory. Particularly in Europe, a deep ambivalence regarding Zionism pervades the public discourse. This ambivalence draws on the complexities of both European-Jewish and European-Muslim relations. It coincides with and strengthens the growing impression that Israel's wars are fought not against near-peer state competitors but, rather, against civilian societies. Through the civilian-victim narrative, Israel's antagonists—Iran, Syria, Hamas, Hezbollah and others—have found a powerful tool for exploiting and exacerbating this ambivalence. They use it to drive a wedge between Europe and Israel. It is a tactic in a long-term diplomatic strategy, as well as in short-term efforts to shift the balance of power in war.

The explosion of new communications technology has given Iran, Syria, Hezbollah, and Hamas a powerful tool for their information strategy. During the Cold War we lived in a deferential information environment. People accepted information as authoritative and legitimate when it was seen to have originated from a person or an organization commanding power and authority in society. In the media world, a handful of newspapers, wire services, and television networks were regarded as titans. Today, by contrast, we live in a referential information aspect of the operating environment. People are more inclined to accept information as authoritative when it is validated by a source—on cable television, on the internet, in the corner market—which they regard as likeminded or wise. This fact gives groups such as Hezbollah and Hamas the ability to influence significant populations with their propaganda.

In a referential information environment, talking points delivered by military spokesmen do not carry as much weight as they did in a deferential age. They are drowned out by the white noise of the new media. They are discounted by foreign populations. They are immediately questioned by NGOs whom the media world regards as impartial and objective.

The adversaries' Strategic Narrative is part of a highly effective military strategy that the Hybrid enemies of Israel (and the United States) will continue to use for years to come. There is no silver bullet that will nullify this strategy. It must be combated by a whole-of-government effort. Within the Army, it requires a full-spectrum approach that integrates all information capabilities and coordinates them fully with combat operations. It also requires a Strategic Narrative. Our message is transmitted by our deeds, whose meaning is reinforced by our words and images; not the other way around. Everything we say and everything we do, and everything we do not say and do not do will influence key relevant audiences and publics in decisive ways. Hybrid War requires developing planning process that will ensure that our actions are calibrated to achieve an information effect.

The US Army's experience of the past decade and its studies of future challenges suggest that maintaining the trust and confidence of home while simultaneously gaining the trust of local publics in the area of hostilities will be as essential to the success of any future Army mission. The Strategic Narrative is an important tool for this effort.

Our authoritarian and terrorist enemies can lie and manipulate, sometimes with devastating effect. The democratic army cannot imitate these practices. The press is very wary of being manipulated by democratic armies (less so of totalitarian and terrorist armies). The best way for the democratic army to influence the media and strategic publics is to develop processes that, through words and actions, will tell a consistent, true, and sincere story.

NOTES

1. Frank G. Hoffman, *Conflict in the 21st Century: The Rise of Hybrid Wars*, (Arlington, VA: Potomac Institute for Policy Studies, December 2007), 14, http://www.potomacinstitute.org/publications/Potomac_HybridWar_0108.pdf.

2. US Army Field Manual 3.0 (Operations) defines: "*Information engagement* is the integrated employment of public affairs to inform US and friendly audiences; psychological operations, combat camera, US Government strategic communication and defense support to public diplomacy, and other means necessary to influence foreign audiences; and, leader and Soldier engagements to support both efforts. Commanders focus their information engagement activities on achieving desired effects locally. However, because land operations always take place in a broader global and regional context, commanders ensure their information engagement plans support and complement those of their higher headquarters, US Government strategic communication guidance when available, and broader US Government policy where applicable."

3. George Packer, "Knowing the Enemy: Can Social Scientists Redefine the 'War on Terror?'" *The New Yorker*, December 18, 2006, 65-66, http://www.newyorker.com/archive/2006/12/18/061218fa_fact2.

4. See Cori E. Dauber, "The Truth Is Out There: Responding to Insurgent Disinformation and Deception Operations", *Military Review*, January-February, 2009, 13-24, http://usacac.army.mil/CAC2/MilitaryReview/Archives/English/MilitaryReview_20090228_art005.pdf.

5. UN General Assembly, *Report of the Secretary-General prepared pursuant to General Assembly Resolution ES-10/10 (Report on Jenin)*, 30 July 2002, http://www.un.org/peace/jenin/.

6. Janine di Giovanni, "Jenin: Lying Down On Broken Glass, Crushing Bones," *The Times*, 16 April 2002, http://www.islamonline.net/english/News/2002-04/16/article40.shtml; quoted in Suzanne Gershowitz and Emanuele Ottolenghi, "Europe's Problem with Ariel Sharon," *Middle East Quarterly*, Fall 2005, Volume XII, Number 4; available at http://www.meforum.org/743/europes-problem-with-ariel-sharon.

7. Sharon Sadeh, "How Jenin Battle Became a 'Massacre,'" *Guardian*, 6 May 2002, http://www.guardian.co.uk/media/2002/may/06/mondaymediasection5.

8. Landes' views can be found on two websites. For his treatment of the al-Durrah affair, see: http://www.seconddraft.org/aldurah.php. For Landes' general critiques of media coverage, see: http://www.theaugeanstables.com/.

9. Barak Ravid, "Government Press Office: Al-Dura's Death Was Staged By Gaza Cameraman," *Haaretz.com*, 2 October 2007, http://www.haaretz.com/hasen/spages/908869.html.

10. "Israel: Gaza Beach Investigation Ignores Evidence," *Human Rights Watch*, 19 June 2006, http://www.hrw.org/en/news/2006/06/19/israel-gaza-beach-investigation-ignores-evidence.

11. See for instance, Ian Fisher and Steven Erlanger, "Botched Israeli Strike Kills Palestinian in Gaza, *New York Times*, 22 June 2006, http://query.nytimes.com/gst/fullpage.html?res=9C02E5DD1F31F931A15755C0A9609C8B63&sec=&spon=.

12. Gerald M. Steinberg, ed., *The NGO Front in the Gaza War, The Durban Strategy Continues* (Jerusalem: NGO Monitor Monograph Series), 2, http://www.ngomonitor.org/data/images/File/NGO_Front_Gaza.pdf.

13. "Full text: Blair on the Media," *BBC News*, http://news.bbc.co.uk/2/hi/uk_news/politics/6744581.stm.

14. Hasan Nasrallah, interview on *al-Manar Television*, 6 June 2000; Quoted in Eyal Zisser, "The Return of Hizbullah," *The Middle East Quarterly*, Fall 2002, Vol. 9, No. 4, http://www.meforum.org/499/the-return-of-hizbullah. See also Daniel Helmer, *Occasional Paper 21— Flipside of the Coin: Israel's Lebanese Incursion Between 1982-2000* (Fort Leavenworth, Kansas: Combat Studies Institute Press, 2007).

15. Roee Nahmias, "Nasrallah: We Won't Be Restrained For A Long Time," *YNetnews.com*, 27 August 2006, http://www.ynetnews.com/articles/0,7340,L-3296420,00.html.

16. Ehud Olmert, "Address by Prime Minister Ehud Olmert—The Knesset," Prime Minister's address to the Knesset, Jerusalem, 17 July 2006, http://www.pmo.gov.il/PMOEng/Archive/Speeches/2006/07/speechknesset170706.htm.

17. Ehud Olmert, "PM Olmert's Remarks At His Press Conference With Japanese PM Junichiro Koizum," Prime Minister's press conference, Jerusalem, 7 December 2006, http://www.pmo.gov.il/PMOEng/Archive/Speeches/2006/07/speechjap120706.htm.

18. "Address by Prime Minister Ehud Olmert—The Knesset."

19. Israeli Comptroller, Report 58A (Annual Report for 2007), 462, http://www.me-

vaker.gov.il/serve/contentTree.asp?bookid=500&id=188&contentid=&parentcid=undefin ed&sw=1024&hw=698.

20. Marvin Kalb, "The Israeli-Hezbollah War of 2006: The Media as a Weapon in Asymmetrical Conflict," Harvard University John F. Kennedy School of Government, 28 February 2007, 19, http://ksgnotes1.harvard.edu/Research/wpaper.nsf/rwp/ RWP07-012.

21. Ibid., 12.

22. "Fatal Strikes: Israel's Indiscriminate Israel's Indiscriminate Attacks Against Civilians in Lebanon," *Human Rights Watch*, 5 September 2006, http://www.hrw.org/ en/news/2007/09/05/israellebanon-israeli-indiscriminate-attacks-killed-most-civilians.

23. Winograd Committee Final Report, Israel Ministry of Foreign Affairs, 30 January 2008, 136.

24. See, for instance: Richard North, "The Corruption of the Media," EU Referendum Blog, entry posted 15 August 2006, http://eureferendum.blogspot.com/2006/08/ corruption-of-media.html.

25. "Why They Died," *Human Rights Watch*, 5 September 2007, 43, http://www. hrw.org/en/reports/2007/09/05/why-they-died.

26. Ibid., 44.

27. A separate inspection team, internal to the military, headed by General Alon Galert, delivered its findings in December 2006. Quotations from Galert team's findings are contained with the 2007 Comptroller's Report.

28. 2007 Comptroller's Report, 461.

29. 2007 Comptroller's Report, 462.

30. 2007 Comptroller's Report, 460.

31. Nadav Eyal, "If Only You Had Been There: The Story of a Foreign Correspondent in the Gaza Strip" *MESI–Middle East Strategic Information*, 20 February 2009, http://www.mesi.org.uk/ViewNews.aspx?ArticleId=2133.

32. See the decision of the Israeli Cabinet, "Procedures for the Work of the Government during Emergencies," http://www.sela.pmo.gov.il/PMO/Archive/Decisions/2008/09/des4065.htm.

33. Hirsh Goodman, "The Effective Public Diplomacy Ended with Operation CAST LEAD," *Jerusalem Post*, 5 February 2009, http://www.jpost.com/servlet/Satell ite?pagename=JPost%2FJPArticle%2FShowFull&cid=1233304700813.

34. Eyal, "If Only You Had Been There;" Goodman, "The Effective Public Diplomacy."

35. Goodman, "The Effective Public Diplomacy."

36. See the *Reuters* video report at: http://www.youtube.com/watch?v=OnEe2N-kxJk; See also Goodman, "The Effective Public Diplomacy."

37. "Summer 2006 Lebanon War: Hezbollah and Israel," *(UNCLASSIFIED/ FOUO)TRISA-Threats*, (Fort Leavenworth, Kansas, 2007), https://www.us.army.mil/ suite/doc/14800506.